SHOOT YOUR NOVEL

Cinematic Techniques to Supercharge Your Writing

C. S. Lakin

CREATE DOC
- Briefly list & detail useful
cinematic techniques collated
from book

Shoot Your Novel: Cinematic Techniques to Supercharge Your
Writing

ISBN-10: 099138945X
ISBN-13: 978-0-9913894-5-2

UBIQUITOUS PRESS

Morgan Hill, CA

Nonfiction Books by C. S. Lakin
The Writer's Toolbox Series

Writing the Heart of Your Story: The Secret to Crafting an Unforgettable Novel

Layer Your Novel: The Innovative Method for Plotting Your Scenes

The 12 Key Pillars of Novel Construction: Your Blueprint for Building a Solid Story

The 12 Key Pillars Workbook

5 Editors Tackle the 12 Fatal Flaws of Fiction Writing

Say What? The Fiction Writer's Handy Guide to Grammar, Punctuation, and Word Usage

Crank It Out! The Surefire Way to Become a Super-Productive Writer

The Memoir Workbook

Other Books

Manipulating the Clock: How Fiction Writers Can Tweak the Perception of Time

Strategic Planning for Writers: 4 Easy Steps to Success

The Memoir Workbook

Praise for *Shoot Your Novel*

"With *Shoot Your Novel*, C. S. Lakin does something wonderful and unique. While lots of us in the business of helping writers and storytellers recommend adding vivid images to scenes, Lakin goes much further to reveal how employing the tools and techniques of movie directing, editing, and cinematography will give your fiction deeper meaning and greater emotional impact. Her book is an essential tool for any serious novelist."

~Michael Hauge, Hollywood screenwriting coach and story consultant, author of *Writing Screenplays That Sell*

"With such an extensive amount of experience in the screenwriting and filmmaking process, it comes as no surprise that C. S. Lakin writes with a trustworthy authority and wealth of insight when it comes to the craft of building dynamic scenes within novels. The pace and flow of *Shoot Your Novel* makes it easy to follow, and the various tips and pointers strewn throughout are succinct. Of particular note is the smart curation of novel excerpts, authors, and filmmakers she cites as examples for the tips she suggests. If you have trouble understanding some of the pointers/tips theoretically, the excerpts always make it more clear.

Having myself adapted *The War of the Roses* for both film and stage (internationally), I can say that I have actually used quite a few of the techniques Lakin discusses, and the one I like the most is the use of portraying "daydreaming" when writing from the POV of a character, effectively blending past, present, and future in one single scene. Well worth the read!"

~Warren Adler, best-selling novelist of *The War of the Roses* and *Random Hearts*

Table of Contents

Introduction

Point and Shoot

So, a man walks into a bar, accompanied by a large piece of asphalt. He goes up to the bartender and says, "I'll have a whiskey." He nods at his friend and adds, "Oh, and one for the road."

If I told this joke to you and a group of your friends, I'm not sure you'd laugh as much as I'd hope, but one thing I am sure of—you would each have pictured this playing out in your head, and each would have seen a completely different "movie." Maybe you pictured this taking place in a Western saloon, with the man dressed in cowboy boots and wearing a Stetson hat. He probably had a Texan drawl, and maybe was chewing tobacco as he spoke. Maybe one of your friends imagined a Yuppie high-end urban bar, with soft leather upholstery and smelling of expensive Cuban cigar smoke.

However you envisioned this briefly described scene, no doubt your friends "saw" something wholly different in their minds. Here's the point: if you had watched this in a movie on the big screen, you and your friends would have seen the exact same things. You wouldn't be arguing later whether the piece of asphalt was black or gray or the man was wearing that hat or not. The film itself provided all the details for you, leaving little to your imagination.

Tell It Like You See It

With fiction, though, writers are presented with an entirely different situation. The reader reading your novel will only see the specifics if you detail them. And even if you do, it's likely she will still envision many of the scene elements different from what you hoped to convey.

That's not necessarily a bad thing. In fact, leaving out details and allowing the reader to "fill in the blanks" is part of the reader-writer relationship. In a way, a novel becomes much more personal than a movie, a little bit of a "choose your own adventure" quality. Many love novels just for that ability to "put themselves" into the story, whether it be by relating to a protagonist, seeing people we know in the characters presented, or feeling like we are going through the trials and perils presented by the plot.

The challenge and beauty of the artistic palette a writer uses raises numerous questions:

- How much or how little detail do I (or should I) put in my novel in order to help the reader see the story the way I see it? And how much should I leave to the reader's imagination?

- How can I best write each scene so that I "show" the reader what I want him to see?

- How can I write scenes that will give the emotional impact equivalent to what can be conveyed through a film?

The joke I told was short and didn't give much detail. It had no power or punch, no strong feel of action or movement. I doubt you will remember it a month from now. Other than the man walking and talking and nodding, the "scene" was stagnant, with little to stir the imagination or evoke emotion.

Maybe your own writing feels this way to you—often—and you don't know what to do to make it better. Maybe you've read a dozen books on writing craft and have attended countless workshops at writers' conferences and you still can't seem to "get" how to write powerful, evocative scenes that move your readers.

Well, if you sometimes feel like strangling, stabbing, or decapitating your novel because of flat, boring, lackluster scenes, you can *shoot* your novel instead!

Show, Don't Tell—But How?

The reading experience is increasingly visual

Sol Stein in his book *Stein on Writing* says, "Twentieth-century readers, transformed by film and TV, are used to *seeing* stories. The reading experience for a twentieth-century reader is increasingly visual. The story is happening in front of his eyes." This is even more true in the twenty-first century. As literary agent and author Donald Maass says in *Writing 21ˢᵗ Century Fiction*: "Make characters do something that readers can visualize."

We've heard it countless times: show, don't tell. Sounds simple, right?

Wrong. There are myriad choices a writer has to make in order to "show" and not "tell" a scene. Writers are often told they need to show, which in essence means to create visual scenes the reader can "watch" unfold as they read.

But telling a writer to "show" is vague. Just how do you show? How do you transfer the clearly enacted scene playing in your mind to the page in a way that not only gets the reader to see just what you want her to see but also comes across with the emotional impact you intend?

The Shotgun Method

Writers know that if they say "Jane was terrified," that only *tells* the reader what Jane is feeling; it doesn't *show* her terrified. So they go on to construct a scene that shows Jane in action and *reacting* to the thing that inspires fear in her. And somehow in doing so writers hope they will make their reader afraid too.

But that's often like using a shotgun approach. You aim at a target from a hundred yards away with a shotgun and hope a few buckshot pellets actually hit the bull's eye.

Many writers think if they just "point and shoot" they will hit their target every time. But then, when they get lackluster reviews, or dozens of agent or publisher rejections, they can't figure out what they did wrong, or failed to do.

Why is this? Is there some "secret formula" to writing visually impacting scenes every time?

No, not secret. In fact, the method is staring writers in the face.

It's Not Really a Secret

We have all been raised watching thousands of movies and television shows. The style, technique, and methods used in film and TV are so familiar to us, we process them comfortably and even subconsciously. We now expect these elements to appear in the novels we read, to some degree—if not consciously then subconsciously.

Filmmaker Gustav Mercado, in his book *The Filmmaker's Eye*, makes this very observation about movies, stating that cinematic tradition has become standardized in the way the rules of composition are applied to certain camera shots "which over time have linked key moments in a story with the use of particular shots." His "novel" approach, which he claims is new, is to examine the shot as "a deeper and discursive exploration into the fundamental elements of the visual language of cinema."

If this has been proven true with camera technique, it stands to reason the same idea would transfer over into writing fiction. If novelists can learn how filmmakers utilize particular camera shots to achieve specific effects, create specific moods, and evoke specific emotions, they have a powerful tool at hand.

We know what makes a great, riveting scene in a movie, and what makes a boring one—at least viscerally. And though our tastes differ, certainly, for the most part we often agree when a scene "works" or doesn't. It either accomplishes what the writer or director has set out to do, or it flops.

So since we have all been (over)exposed to film and its visual way of storytelling, and its influence on society has altered the tastes of fiction readers, it's only logical to take a look at what makes a great movie. Note that we're not looking at plot or premise in this book, for that's an entirely different subject. Instead, we're going to deconstruct movie technique into bite-sized pieces.

Just as your novel comprises a string of scenes that flow together to tell your whole story, so too with movies and television shows. However, you, the novelist, lay out your scenes much differently from the way a screenwriter does. Whereas you might see each of your scenes as integrated, encapsulated moments of time, a movie director sees each scene as a compilation of a number of *segments or pieces*—a collection of camera shots that are subsequently edited and fit together to create that seamless "moment of time."

Time to Put On a New Hat

So take off your writer hat for a minute and put on a director one—you know, that sun visor you see the director wear as he's looking through the camera eyepiece on the outdoor set of the big studio lot and as he considers how he's going to shoot the next scene.

Have you ever watched a behind-the-scenes look at how a movie is being filmed, or a TV series? I love watching and listening to Peter Jackson in his many videos detailing the filming of both *The Lord of the Rings* and *The Hobbit* feature films. Jackson does a wonderful job showing the kinds of decisions he has to make as he ponders the shooting of a scene in order to get across the impact, mood, details, and key moments he desires in the final cut.

Directors have to plan like this. They can't show up on the set each morning and look at the shooting schedule and just "wing it." A large sum of money is riding on the director doing his homework and knowing exactly what each scene must convey and show to the viewer. Directors decide just how a scene will be shown and what specifically will be focused on. Using the camera, a director can basically "force" viewers to see exactly what he wants them to see. And one goal in doing this is to evoke a particular emotional reaction from them.

Writing Is Not All That Different from Directing

Writers can do the same. They may not be able to paint so specific a picture that every single reader will envision a novel exactly the same—and that's a good thing. In fact, that's what makes reading novels so ... well, novel. Readers infuse their personalities, backgrounds, fears, and dreams into a book as they read. A character named Tiffany will conjure up a face for me different from the one you picture in your head. In this way, novels are an interactive experience—the reader's imagination interacting with the novelist's.

Yet, writers can also put on their director's hat—and well they should. Remember, readers nowadays want to read books that are more visual, as Stein remarked—scenes that are happening right before their eyes. But few writers are ever shown just how to do this effectively, and that's what this book is about. You don't have to guess anymore how to "show" a scene in a way that's "supercharged." By learning to use camera shots the way a director does, you too can take readers where you want them to go, make them see what you want them to see. Don't leave that up to the reader to decide. Be not just the writer but the director.

Filmmaker Gustav Mercado makes a succinct point in his book: "You should not be subservient to the dictates of a technique but make the technique work for the specific needs of your story instead." What a great truth for both novelists and filmmakers.

So get out of your cozy office chair and follow me onto the set where all the great movies are filmed. Get out your writer's toolbox and be prepared to add a whole new layer of tools: camera shots. Once you learn what these are and how to use them in writing fiction, it's more than likely you will never write the same way again—or look at a scene the same way.

And I truly hope so. I hope once you grab these cinematic secrets and supercharge your novel, you will never take that shotgun out again and just "point and shoot." Instead, you will be the director looking at the scene from all angles and making deliberate decisions regarding which camera angles to use for the greatest impact.

Chapter 1

It's All about the Angle

Having spent my entire childhood at the feet of my screenwriter mother, I read more TV scripts than books while growing up, as there were piles of them around my mother's office, and I'd often curl up on the couch and read one after school. I also spent many hours on sound stages and on location watching many of her TV episodes being filmed. Okay, I will confess I liked to sit in Peggy Lipton's chair during the shooting of *Mod Squad*, and if we were outside I wore my mirror shades to be in sync with the dynamic threesome I admired (I rarely saw Clarence Williams III ever take his shades off—indoors or outdoors).

I spent many hours wandering in and out of sound stages at Fox, MGM, and other studios where my mother, for a time, had an office. I'd sneak into *M.A.S.H* and watch the banter Alan Alda tossed around as he operated on a fake body in the surgery tent, or mosey on over to *Battlestar Gallactica*. I had fun going on location and even spent a week in San Francisco on the set with Rock Hudson (*MacMillan and Wife*), since my stepfather was the director of that episode, and got to watch some cool stunts involving cable cars (no, Rock didn't do his own stunts!).

I say all this to make the point that growing up in a home that centered on writing and directing for television greatly influenced the way I approach storytelling. Ever since I learned the alphabet, I wrote stories. I even pitched my first script idea at age twelve to the producer of *The Girl from U.N.C.L.E.* Do you remember that show? (Okay just so you know, Stephanie Powers starred in it, and Ian Fleming was the consultant on the show and suggested the idea, but it only ran twenty-nine episodes before being canceled for low ratings. Maybe if they had bought my idea and wrote that script, it wouldn't have failed. Hmm, I wonder. . .)

I still have my very polite rejection letter—my first of many! It did help that my mother was a staff writer on the show and had "an in." However, they didn't buy my idea. But you can be sure of one thing— even at age twelve I presented my idea to the producer in a way he could easily visualize it as an episode. My young mind was already programmed to write cinematically.

So when I began writing novels decades later (although I promised my mother I would never be a writer, but that's another story), it was only natural for me to construct all my scenes visually, the way I might see them play out on film. In fact, I couldn't imagine writing any differently.

I'm not surprised when I continually get comments from readers like: "I could so picture this book as a movie" or "this novel would make a great movie." I believe they say these things not so much because they think my books are brilliant but because I write *cinematically*. Every scene is structured either consciously or unconsciously with a series of camera shots, so the reader will see the scene play out the way *I* see it.

I'm very familiar with the camera shots used—and as I mentioned before, you really are too. If you've watched a few TV shows or seen a few movies, you're already familiar with what I'm going to share with you.

What you don't yet know, possibly, is how to *transcribe* what you see on the screen to the words on your pages. So I'm going to deconstruct movie technique by examining the camera shots one by one, and showing examples in novels in which the author has effectively used a particular camera angle (or multiple angles) to create a supercharged scene.

Varieties of Camera Angles for Specific Effects

Screenplays are structured through the use of camera direction, which becomes all-important to telling the story. The choice of camera angles within a scene affects the mood, focus, and emphasis of the story being told, and directs the viewer to pay attention to particular elements unfolding. The right camera angle will give the best impact:

you wouldn't film a huge explosion using a Close-Up but rather a Long Shot encompassing the wide scope of action.

Writers, too, should think about not just the character POV (point of view) of a scene but the camera angles. Don't leave it up to the reader to figure out what is important to notice. Put on your director's hat and think what shots will focus on what's important. By using these filming techniques to point your reader's attention where *you* want it to go, you will get the results you want.

Don't Be Boring

Most authors use the same angle in every scene, and that can be boring. What do I mean by "the same angle"? I mean that if there were a camera filming what was taking place in the scene, it would be set up in one spot and never move. It would never zoom in, pan, pull back, or follow anyone.

Is that bad? Not necessarily. You may have a scene that is solely in a character's head—just her thinking. And maybe that's a powerful scene because of the character and plot points revealed. But would you enjoy reading a book in which most of the scenes were like that? Probably not. In fact, if you read a few pages of explanation and internal thinking and *nothing was happening* (read: no real-time playing out of a scene you can visualize), you just might throw the book down and go get a bowl of ice cream to soothe your battered soul.

It's Just Not Happening

Haven't you read scenes in which two people are sitting somewhere (and you've probably not been told where) and just talking? The dialog goes on for pages, and maybe some of it is interesting, but you can't picture where these people are, what the setting is like, what they look like. Or maybe you have more description than you want—of the restaurant and their clothes and hair and the noise and smells inside. But still—nothing *happens*.

I'm not talking about physical action. And this is an important distinction. There can be a lot happening in a scene without a character even twitching. There can be heavy subtext, innuendo, clues, suspicions—all kinds of tension and plot reveals going on. But still, the scene can feel flat and a bit boring because it feels as if the camera filming all this is stuck in one spot across the room.

This is not to say every scene needs to have your "camera" zooming and panning and doing gymnastics to keep your reader's interest up. But once you see how you can bring in a variety of camera shots to your scenes—even the ones in which not much is happening—you will realize there are better ways to construct them to supercharge them.

Don't settle for okay or boring or so-so. Think *big impact*. That's what great directors do. And big impact doesn't apply to just explosive scenes with high action. You can have a huge-impact small moment. A tiny element in your story can be key—the gripping linchpin upon which your entire plot hinges—and by using the right camera shots, you can play up that subtle bit and blow it up to the size it should be. High-impact moments, regardless of how subtle, should "fill the entire screen." And I'll show you how it can be done.

The Art of Film Editing

Have you ever watched old black-and-white movies? I'm thinking in particular of those great Fred Astaire musicals full of amazing dance routines. Sometime, go watch a few and pay attention to the camera shot. Back in the day, film editing was kept to a minimum. It was expensive, tedious work. Film editors had to literally cut and splice pieces of film together, which was tricky to do seamlessly. Because of this, most of those great dance numbers are one long shot from one camera, without interruptions, without slicing and dicing. Not like what's done today. It makes me wonder how many takes Fred and Ginger had to do to get one good keeper shot. I get tired just thinking about all those fast, nifty steps.

Today, editing is a highly praised art form, and with the current tech is much easier and versatile. A film editor must creatively work with the layers of images, story, dialogue, music, pacing, as well as the actors' performances to effectively "re-imagine" and even rewrite the film to craft a cohesive whole. Editors usually play a dynamic role in the making of a film. Walter Murch once said, "Film editing is now something almost everyone can do at a simple level and enjoy it, but to take it to a higher level requires the same dedication and persistence that any art form does."

The editing in film often goes unnoticed. However, if one does not notice the editing, then it is doing its job. The editor works on the subconscious of the viewer, and if you think about it, writers do the same when they write a novel. Editors are awarded Academy Awards, and maybe you've wondered why, but I don't.

Now, you may think it really odd, but knowing my background, you should understand when I say one of the things I pay the most attention to when I watch a movie (and comment on to my husband—to which he can attest!) is the editing. I feel the editing is what makes the movie. A terrifically edited movie scores more points in my "book" than a well-written one. I am enthralled when I watch a beautifully edited movie, when all the cuts of the various camera shots are pieced together like a symphony.

One movie that comes to mind is *Inception*. There are sequences in that movie that are edited to show reality unfolding on three different dream levels all at the same time. It is masterfully done. If you've watched the opening scene of *Saving Private Ryan* and you felt like your heart was being ripped out, much of that was due to the brilliant, powerful editing. Although I could barely view the painful images on the screen (and I'm glad I saw it on my small TV and not in a theater), I can't forget specific camera angles used, such as the shot taken from the seaward side of the landing craft looking toward the beach as the Allied soldiers try to disembark and are mowed down with machine-gun fire, many while still in the boat, the water turning red as bodies keep falling.

In contrast, a movie with boring editing will tend to show boring scenes that feel flat or choppy or lacking spark.

Yes, Another Hat

If you haven't figured out by now where I'm going with this, I hope you won't be surprised to have me tell you that, yes, you also need to wear that editor's hat. I don't mean the "book" kind of editor, like me, but the movie kind I mentioned above—the person who takes the film of all the raw footage of the shot scenes and pieces it together in not just the right order but in a specific sequence.

EDITOR

Think about it. Each scene in a movie or TV show is not just shot from one angle; it's shot from many. There are close shots in which you see one character's face and the back of another's head. There are stationary shots taken from different angles, as well as numerous moving shots taken from different angles. You may have an aerial shot, some long shots, some tilted ones, some tracking shots done with the camera moving along on a dolly.

The director will make clear which shots he wants. He then, along with various producers and others, will work with the film editor to choose which shots to use in a scene, and like a jigsaw puzzle will (hopefully) seamlessly put it together so it flows without lagging, as well as provides just the right tension and pacing needed.

It's not easy. And novelists have to do exactly the same thing. They have to not only "shoot" their scenes, they have to choose the camera angles, and then piece it all together in a way that fits their genre and story, and keeps the pacing going at the speed needed to engage the reader. A novel set in Victorian England showing the characters having tea and discussing suitable marriage prospects (not my cup of tea) should have different camera shots and entirely different editing than a suspense thriller in which the protagonist has to save the world before the ticking bomb explodes.

CUT TO: An Important Point

I want to say "cut" here to emphasize something I need to talk about and will reiterate throughout this book, and that's the importance of being aware of the "high moment" of each of your scenes. This is what good directors know. Before they shoot that scene on their shooting schedule for the day, they are thinking about that instant (whether it will last a few seconds or even a minute) the scene is building to.

Without going into a treatise about scene construction (which I do in my book *Writing the Heart of Your Story*), suffice it to say each scene must have a point to it or it shouldn't be in your novel. If you have scenes with no "point," you need to either give them a point or throw them out. Too many writers write too many scenes with no point to them.

Filmmaker Gustav Mercado says to create powerful impact, the technical elements, compositional choices, and narrative content should all work in context to create *meaning*. Without meaning, what is the point of telling your story?

Ever seen a movie that left you scratching your head? A movie with scenes that had no point to them, and for the life of you, you couldn't figure out why they were in the movie at all? Same thing. Someone should have cut those scenes out or rewritten them, you think. Maybe you've said that about scenes you've read in some novels too. Hopefully no one has said that about your novels, but if they have, you can fix that. How? By making sure you have a high moment you are building to in every scene.

A high moment doesn't have to be a huge moment. Remember, what's significant to a reader is *what impacts the character*. Just a single word can pack a punch in a scene, and often does. A beautifully delivered line of dialog can be more explosive than blowing up the Statue of Liberty. Great movie directors know this too. As actress Rosalind Russell said, what makes a great movie is "moments." And in order to write supercharged scenes that utilize specific camera shots, you have to know what moment you are building to. Just keep that in mind.

A String of Shots Equals a Scene

Movies are made up of a string of shot sequences—don't confuse these with whole scenes. In creating a shot sequence, the aim of using a camera is to imitate the way the human mind uses the eyes. Our minds will not let our eyes stay fixed on any one subject for more than four or five seconds. Our eyes are constantly moving and focusing on different subjects.

For example, you may be walking down the street and you come across two of your friends having a small picnic at one of the tables in the city park at the corner. Your mind will probably direct your eyes into the following views of the couple:

- First, you would have a Wide-Angle or Long Shot of the entire scene.

- As you walk toward the couple, you will look at one person, and then the other.

- As you come closer, you might shift your focus and look at what is on the table.

- Your next glance will probably be at the first person who speaks to you.

- As the conversation continues, your eyes will shift from person to person, from person to table, from an action of one person to that person's face etc., etc. The combinations could be endless.

This type of realistic behavior is what you want to capture in your fiction writing, and the way to do it is by utilizing various camera angles—the difference being that you have a *specific intention* in doing so.

Rather than show a random encounter with boring dialog and nothing all that interesting happening in the scene—which is what real life often is like—you have an objective in playing this scene out, that high point you are leading to, a moment of revelation or plot twist that is going to deliver with a punch when you reach it.

And so every camera angle is used deliberately to give the most punch when needed.

Television producers follow a basic rule that no shot should last more than thirty seconds, and no scene should last longer than three minutes. This is the 30-3 Rule. This is the basic idea of how shot sequences are made. You take one long scene and break it down into a variety of short shots.

How does this translate to fiction? A scene can take much longer than three minutes to read, and sometimes it may cover a number of moments in time, some even separated by days and weeks. But if you break down your scenes and look at the segments that take place, you will find a natural rhythm that feels just right.

Scenes should be mini novels, with a beginning, middle, and end. It doesn't work to place strict rules on scenes, for they should be as long as they need to be—whatever it takes to effectively reveal the bit of storyline intended while keeping the pacing and tension taut. However, I believe if you lay out your scenes intentionally with a series of camera shots, leaving out excessive narration and backstory, your scenes will "move" like a movie and will feel like concise, succinct movie scenes.

Two Types of Camera Shots

Essentially, there are two types of camera shots—stationary and moving. I've never seen them classified this way, so I use these terms I came up with. Or you could think of them as static and dynamic, or still and kinetic. Use whatever terms work for you. But basically we're talking about filming a moment in which the camera is either moving or not moving. Simple.

You decide which types of camera shots you will use based on your high moment. If the high point of your scene involves showing an expression on someone's face, an object (like a ring), a small detail not before noticed, then the key camera shot will be a Close-Up (CU), which might also be called a Close Shot. If the high moment will be a sudden massive explosion due to an unnoticed gas leak, the key moment will require a Pull Back (PB) and/or a Long Shot (LS). By knowing the key moment and how your plot builds to it, you can plan the camera angles to best enhance the visual experience and evoke the strongest emotional reaction from your reader.

Of course, your scenes have more to them than just the high moment, and for that reason, you will need to use a number of camera angles for each scene, for the most part. But I bring up the need to first identify your high moment and determine what shot is needed *then*, for that's the moment of greatest impact and needs the most emphasis.

Once you know how you will show that moment, you can work backward and forward, figuring out the rest of the shots. This is just my method. I have no idea if movie directors think this way or plan each scene out in any particular fashion. Maybe some work chronologically, deciding on the first shot and going from there. But I believe if you use this method, it will best serve you and the needs of your plot.

So as we go through these stationary and moving camera shots, think about when you might want to keep the "camera still" and when you want to move it from one place to another. As you will see, there's a specific purpose to each shot.

Part 1

Stationary Camera Shots

---

12 MONKEYS

Written by Dave Peoples and Janet Peoples, 1995
Directed by Terry Gilliam
Film Edited by Mick Audsley

INT. WARD DAYROOM – MORNING

ANGLE ON TV SCREEN/A VIDEO IMAGE OF A LAB
MONKEY, convulsing pathetically, a victim of
shocks from the numerous wires attached to his
tiny, restrained body.

ANGLE ON COLE, sitting, writing intensely in a
magazine with crayon, surrounded by dull-eyed
PATIENTS in pajamas and ratty robes, staring at
the shuddering LAB MONKEY on the TV screen.

                    JEFFREY'S VOICE (o.s.)
        Torture! Experiments! We're all monkeys

COLE looks up, startled, as JEFFREY, one eye
bruised black, takes the seat next to him.

                    COLE
            They hurt you!

                        JEFFREY
     Not as bad as what they're doing to
     kitty.

ANGLE ON TV, showing a laboratory CAT turning
in mad circles, eating its own tail, while a
NEWS REPORTER narrates.

                    TV NEWS REPORTER (v.o.)
          These video tapes were obtained by
          animal rights activists who worked
          underground as laboratory assistants
          for several months. Authorities say
          there is little they can do until...

The video footage now shows LAB WORKERS
watching the results of their experiments
passively.

ANGLE ON COLE, reacting angrily.

                        COLE
          Look at those assholes, they're asking
          for it! Maybe people deserved to be
          wiped out!

                        JEFFREY
                 (startled, turning)
          Wiping cut the human race! That's a
          great idea! But it's more of a long
          term thing—right now we have to
          focus on more immediate goals.
                 (sudden whisper)
          I didn't say a word about "you know
          What."

                        COLE
          What are you talking about???
                        JEFFREY
             You know—your plan.

As COLE stares, befuddled, JEFFREY sees COLE'S
magazine.

> JEFFREY
> What're you writing? You a reporter?

> COLE
> (shielding the magazine)
> It's private.

> JEFFREY
> A lawsuit? You going to sue them?

Just then BILLINGS looms over COLE, extending a
cup full of pills.

> BILLINGS
> Yo, James—time to take your meds.

Stationary camera shots are the staple of most movies and TV episodes. We see life most often as if looking through a stationary camera, whether close up on what we are viewing or far away. These essential shots define our world, whether the real one around us or the imaginary one we are putting down on paper. We are not always moving, nor does our gaze continually move without letup. So as we explore the different stationary camera shots, keep in mind the types of moments in a scene that will need a camera focused steadily and unmoving for best effect.

Chapter 2

Setting Up the Scene

Establishing Shot

Establishing Shots are critical in a film. They clue the viewer where this next scene is about to take place. Each time the location of a scene shifts, a new Establishing Shot does exactly what its name implies: it *establishes* where the story will now continue, and fiction writers need to do the same thing.

The purpose is to give a general impression rather than specific information. Often a Long Shot is used for an Establishing Shot, but not all Long Shots *are* Establishing Shots, so those will be discussed in another chapter. Although Establishing Shots are mostly used at the beginning of a scene to set the locale, they can also be used at the end of a segment to provide a revealing or unexpected context, which can pack a big punch when offering the audience a surprising twist tied into the setting or landscape.

So often beginning novelists will start their scenes with dialog or narrative that assumes the reader knows where the characters are. But really, we readers have no clue unless the author clues us in. If nothing is said to indicate otherwise, readers will figure this new scene is a continuation of the previous one. So it's essential that as you move from scene to scene, you not only make clear the time that has passed since the last scene but also the locale. Perhaps the locale hasn't changed at all, but it's now nighttime instead of noon. Do you still need an Establishing Shot? Yes—at least to make it clear we are in the same place but hours or days later.

A Brief Few Seconds

Watch some TV episodes or movies and pay attention to these Establishing Shots (ES). Each time there's a shift of locale, the first few seconds will let you know exactly where the scene is going to take place, whether it be on board the Death Star in *Star Wars* or in the kitchen in *Downton Abbey*. Before Sherlock starts telling Watson to pay attention to the lady holding the parasol, we first see the dirty backstreets of London on a drizzly gray day. The Establishing Shot should only show what is important and relative to the scene and is best if shown from the POV character's eyes and tainted by her mood.

In a film or TV show, the opening Establishing Shot lasts maybe three to four seconds. So in translating into fiction, you don't want more than a paragraph or two. Writers can get away with an omniscient POV in these instances. Imagine the camera far away, revealing the setting, locale, and weather.

You want to be careful to not slip into boring narration, so keep the ES short—a "nod to setting," as author Elizabeth George says. Sometimes only a sentence is needed if the reader has already been to this particular location you have just moved your character to. But using an Establishing Shot is important, for you don't want to confuse your readers. Unless you have a reason to.

Here's a great example of an Establishing Shot beginning in an omniscient storytelling manner—just a few paragraphs—in order to set the mood and scene before introducing the main characters and diving into the close-up dialog and playing out of the scene. Notice how David Baldacci, here in his novel *Sixth Man*, does this smoothly, without dull, detached narrative.

The small jet bumped down hard on the runway in Portland, Maine. It rose up in the air and banged down again harder. Even the pilot was probably wondering if he could keep the twenty-five-ton jet on the tarmac. Because he was trying to beat a storm in, the young aviator had made his approach at a steeper trajectory and a faster speed than the airline's manual recommended. The wind shear culled off the leading edge of the cold front had caused the jet's wings to pendulum back and forth. The copilot had warned the passengers that the landing would be bumpy and a bit more than uncomfortable.

He'd been right. . . . [more description of the tenuous landing follows]

One man, however, merely woke when the plane transitioned off the runway and onto the taxiway to the small terminal. The tall dark-haired woman sitting next to him idly stared out the window, completely unfazed by the turbulent approach and bouncy touchdown.

After they'd arrived at the gate and the pilot shut down the twin GE turbofans, Sean Kind and Michelle Maxwell rose and grabbed their bags from the overhead. As they threaded out through the narrow aisle along with the other deplaning passengers, a queasy-looking woman behind them said, "Boy, that sure was a rough landing."

Sean looked at her, yawned, and massaged his neck. "Was it?"

And from this point on we are in Sean's POV, and the story is off and running. An effective introduction.

So think about times where you may want to achieve this same effect, which gives the reader a nice "big picture" of the setting before being immersed in the characters and the flow of the particular scene.

When You Want to Be Vague

Ever seen a horror movie in which a scene starts and all you see is a dark figure or a gloved hand turning a knob? Perhaps the scene goes on a few minutes as the seedy-looking character ambles down an obscured hallway, and you have no clue who or where he is. No doubt, the writer intended you to be kept (literally) in the dark. That's in keeping with the genre and the writer's intention. And you may have scenes in your novel in which you want to accomplish the same thing. So then, leave out an Establishing Shot, if that's your aim. Or keep it vague on purpose.

But if it's not your intention to be vague or confusing, think twice about starting a scene with pages of dialog between characters without setting up where and when they are. At some point the reader will scratch her head, flip pages, and try to figure out just where these people are. And that's not a good thing.

Remember, a novel is not a visual experience unless you make it one. Unlike a movie, you could spend three hundred pages solely inside a character's head without ever showing his world. In fact, your character could be blind, and if you are an exceptionally adept writer, you could write a riveting book without ever "showing" anything visual and relying on thought and other senses to carry the plot and tell your story (there's a challenge for you). The visuals, then, are the writer's responsibility, and they must be specifically chosen for effect.

Filter It through Your Character

Every scene in a movie, however, is *seen*, and so the screenwriter must choose *what* the viewer will see and from *what* angle. And unless the director is using the camera angle POV (which we'll examine later), what is seen is a bit detached from the main character in the scene.

However, with novels, you always want to try to show a scene through the POV character's eyes and colored by her emotions, state of mind, and way of thinking.

An Establishing Shot is a great place to immediately plunge the reader into your character's frame of mind, and a perfect example of a powerful Establishing Shot in a novel is this one from John Le Carré's *The Constant Gardener*.

Le Carré does a terrific job coloring this shot with the use of appropriate adjectives and his choice of words. Keep in mind that his protagonist, Justin Quayle, is (literally) on a dangerous journey trying to discover the details of his wife's death, which he suspects will turn out to be a murder.

The Establishing Shot reflects Justin's state of mind, and it nicely sets the mood for the scene unfolding. It's clear every word was chosen carefully. If you think writing a paragraph or two introducing the setting and time of your scene can only be boring, think again.

The mountain stood black against the darkening sky, and the sky was a mess of racing cloud, perverse island winds and February rain. The snake road was strewn with pebbles and red mud from the sodden hillside. Sometimes it became a tunnel of overhanging pine branches and sometimes it was a precipice with a free fall to the steaming Mediterranean a thousand feet below. He would make a turn and for no reason the sea would rise in a wall in front of him, only to fall back into the abyss as he made another. But no matter how many times he turned, the rain came straight at him, and when it struck the windscreen he felt the jeep wince under him like an old horse no longer fit for heavy pulling.

Look at some of the words he uses: *black, darkening* (his quest to find answers is getting that way), *perverse* (that too), *winds, rain, snake, sodden, tunnel, precipice* . . . I don't need to go on—you get the point. The Establishing Shot in this scene was no doubt chosen to work as a metaphor, as the reader has been watching Justin Quayle going through a similar emotional roller coaster, rising and falling into an abyss, turning one way then another, but getting nowhere fast. His task to find answers feels like he's prodding "an old horse no longer fit for heavy pulling." And the weight he is carrying is heavy. Powerful, right?

That's all Le Carré needs to start the scene, and from there we move on to other camera shots revealing important plot points leading to a high moment in his scene. I won't tell you what that is; you can read it for yourself, and I hope you do. Few writers handle words as masterfully and deliberately as does Le Carré, and he's a great author to study for cinematic structure.

A Tease before Establishing the Setting

Take a look at this Establishing Shot from the movie *Jurassic Park*, written by Michael Crichton and directed by Steven Spielberg. Notice how Crichton uses an Extreme Close-Up to show minute detail, teasing the audience with the imagery shown in the opening moments. He then switches to a more traditional Establishing Shot to ground the locale for the start of the story.

EXTREME CLOSEUP of glowing honey-colored stones. Their shapes ABSTRACT as THE CAMERA EXAMINES air bubbles and crystalline patterns.

MOVING UP AND OVER this amber abstraction, the CAMERA FINDS unusual shapes and imperfections caught in the glassy stone: flecks of dirt, hairs, cracks. STILL MOVING. STARBURSTS OF LIGHT ricochet off the different surfaces of the stones.

CAMERA TURNS along a creamy stretch of amber. IT TURNS IN DEEPER, abstracting the picture further only to find A TINY BLUR that suddenly RACKS INTO FOCUS - a bug, a mosquito lodged within an amber tomb. It is folded on its back.

SLOW MOTION as the tip of a fine-pointed drill bores into the amber toward the trapped bug. Orange flecks fly. The mosquito trembles. The drill continues, stopping just before it touches the tiny body.

A SHINY PAIR of thin needle-nose pliers reach in the borehole and extricate the mosquito remains. These are dropped on a brightly lit glass slide. A conveyor belt starts, and the slide moves along, arriving under a long-lensed microscope.

IN MICROSCOPIC PERSPECTIVE, a thin needle pierces the bug and delicately removes a fragment of tissue.

PINCERS snare the fragment, dropping it into a narrow tube. The tube SPINS, faster and faster until it is a BLUR on the screen.

THE SCREEN FLOODS with an INFRA-RED LIGHT. Gray oval shapes rock in a neutral mist.

WASH OUT TO:

HOT SUN overhead in a BIG SKY -

EXT BADLANDS - AFTERNOON

Lodged in the cracked earth are the partially-exposed fossilized remains of A VELOCIRAPTER, a carnivorous dinosaur. WIDEN OUT to a SWEEPING PANORAMA of a dinosaur dig, a major excavation filled with workers shoveling earth and stone, making measurements, taking photographs,

```
scribbling  notes,  and  conferring  with  each
other.

The  center  of  all  this  activity  is  one  man.  In
a  roped-off  area  that  circumscribes  the  exposed
bones  of  the  raptor  is  DR.  ALAN  GRANT,  head
paleontologist.  Good-looking,  late  30's,  with  a
thin  beard.

Grant  lies  on  his  belly,  completely  absorbed  in
a  small  piece  of  bone.  A  GROUP  OF  TWELVE
STUDENTS,  notebooks  in  hand,  await  his  next
sentence.

CLOSE  ON  -  the  tiny  bone.  Grant's  nose  touches
it.

Grant  brushes  the  bone  with  a  toothbrush.  Then
he  decides  on  a  quicker  way  to  clean  it.  He
licks  it.  Excited  by  his  discovery,  he  gets  to
his  feet  and  addresses  his  students,  who  listen
raptly.
```

Notice how Crichton makes a dramatic shift from the detail of a tiny bug trapped in amber to a "sweeping panorama" of the dinosaur dig. He quickly shows just where the first true scene will unfold, then locks on to his main character for the scene: Dr. Grant. Without wasting any time, the viewer is drawn into action, with Dr. Grant finding a bone and showing it to his students. How much time is spent establishing the scene? Very little. Perhaps under a minute of screen time. But it's enough to do just what needs to be done: *establish* where this scene is taking place.

If you've read the novel, you may recall it doesn't start with these scenes at all. In fact, the scene introducing the dig begins at page thirty-four, and doesn't quite have the punch of Crichton's screenplay (he wrote both). Take a look at the novel version:

Visitors found the badlands depressingly bleak, but when Grant looked at this landscape he saw something else entirely. This barren land was what remained of another, very different world which had vanished eighty million years ago. In his mind's eye, Grant saw himself back in the warm, swampy bayou that formed the shoreline of a great inland sea.

Crichton goes on with a few paragraphs of backstory and exposition that may or may not be interesting to the reader, and which ends with telling he's in northern Montana. Then we hear someone calling his name, and we get this as the true Establishing Shot:

He stood, a barrel-chested, bearded man of forty. He heard the chugging of the portable generator, and the distant clatter of the jackhammer cutting into the dense rock on the next hill. He saw the kids working around the jackhammer, moving away the big pieces of rock after checking them for fossils. At the foot of the hill, he saw six tipis of his camp, the flapping mess tent, and the trailer that served as their field laboratory. And he saw Ellie waving to him, from the shadow of the field laboratory.

From there, Ellie yells that there's a visitor, and Grant's attention shifts to the blue truck driving over the rutted road kicking up dust as it heads toward him.

Just Enough Details, Then Move On

Crichton doesn't spend pages detailing the weather—only a hint of wind flapping the tipis (although I always feel giving a bit of the weather and time of day/time of year helps fix the character more specifically in the setting) or describing how many students are digging, what they're wearing, what the fossils look like. Crichton wants to get the reader *into the action* of the scene, and he knows most people will have a general feel for what an archaeological dig might look like. He leaves those details for the reader's imagination to fill in.

What he does choose is a touch of sensory detail—sound. Just mentioning the jackhammer and the generator gives texture and implies much. A generator means they are too far from civilization to tap into local power lines. A jackhammer implies hard labor and a forceful attack on nature. Serious hard work. Important work. Six tipis means he has a good-sized crew, and they are roughing it out in the badlands. No fancy RVs here, but they're "kids" to his protagonist, who is forty years old, which shows how his main character is seeing what's going on around him.

Again, Crichton gives just enough detail to establish the shot *through his POV character's eyes*, then moves onto what's important—building to the high moment of the scene. If you don't remember what that is, you can grab a copy of the novel and read it. But it will be there, as Crichton was a master at scene structure and made sure every scene had a purpose in advancing his plot.

It's Okay to Start with Omniscient POV

As mentioned earlier, Establishing Shots in a novel are sometimes the only "acceptable" place to shift into an omniscient POV for a brief time. You may want to open with an aerial shot and zoom into a small street in a small town, or follow a bird as it flies down to a bird feeder outside the home of your protagonist. Novelists can get away with a little touch of detached camera effect before immersing the reader in their POV character's head.

Back in the day, many fine novels unfolded this way, and John Steinbeck excelled in this method. In *The Grapes of Wrath*, he used the complete, short first chapter in an omniscient viewpoint to set the stage for the book. Then, in chapter 2, he ambled his way into action, eventually pulling out of that storytelling voice and into his protagonist's POV. We watch a scene where Joad walks over to a diner and gets a lift from a truck driver, and through active dialog loaded with plenty to help the reader learn just who Joad is, setting up the tone, voice, and plot goals for the novel, Steinbeck shifts into action.

However, in this century, as I mentioned in the opening chapter, readers don't want to spend pages reading narrative and description. They want to see scenes played out in real time, with something happening right away that grabs them and gets them into the head of the characters. Some literary novelists with their evocative writing may be able to get away with pages of narrative. By infusing a scene with internal conflict and mystery, they may successfully rivet their readers without "shooting" the scene—or many scenes—at all.

Certainly those types of books can become best sellers and are often highly acclaimed. But since today's reader is so accustomed to seeing stories on the screen, you may opt to lean more toward a cinematic approach and keep your Establishing Shot short and succinct so that you can move from there into the meat of the scene.

Chapter 3

Determining the Detail with Three Basic Distances

The Close-Up

THE BIRDS

Screenplay by Evan Hunter, 1962
Adapted from the novel by Daphne DeMaurier

FULL SHOT - MELANIE'S OPEN CAR - (MATTE)

on the coast highway. It is a spectacularly
beautiful day, with a cloudless blue sky. The
montage of SHOTS that follow should alternate
between the winding, twisting road and the
ocean below, and CLOSE-UPS of Melanie driving
with the caged birds on the seat beside her.
The last shot should be a FULL SHOT of the car
rounding a particularly sharp curve.

CLOSE SHOT - MELANIE

She turns wheel forcefully.

CLOSE SHOT - THE LOVEBIRDS

in the cage as the car rounds the bend. They
lean to one side as the car turns, come up
straight again as the car rounds the curve.

FULL SHOT - (MATTE)

Car approaching Bodega Bay seen high up.

CLOSE SHOT - MELANIE

at the wheel, she glances out toward the bay.

FULL SHOT - A CLUSTER OF BUILDINGS AT
WATERFRONT

ahead, through the windshield as the car
approaches.

CLOSE SHOT - MELANIE

behind the wheel, leaning forward slightly for
a look at the town.

LONG SHOT - DOCKS ON LEFT

through the windshield as Melanie slows her
speed.

CLOSE SHOT - MELANIE

behind wheel.

LONG SHOT - STORES

on right of the road as Melanie enters the
town. SLOW PAN matching car's cruise past
BAKERY, SHOE REPAIR, CLEANERS, RADIO AND
TELEVISION.

CLOSE SHOT - MELANIE

behind wheel.

LONG SHOT - THE TIDES

past the gas station and beyond to the parking area and the docks, continuing Melanie's slow observation of the place.

CLOSE SHOT - MELANIE - (PROCESS)

studying the town. The car turns into road by gas station.

FULL SHOT - THE TOWN

through the windshield. The car turns right. There is life in the town now, fishermen crossing the road, women with their hair in curlers, old ladies carrying shopping bags. This is Saturday morning, and the town—such as it is—is alive with its inhabitants. We see them from Melanie's P.O.V. AS SHE SCANS THE PLACE FOR ITS POST OFFICE. (THIS TO BE TAKEN ON BACK LOT.)

FULL SHOT - THE CAR

pulling in, in front of the post office. Melanie opens the door and steps out. She is smartly dressed in a traveling suit and sweater. She looks up at the sign, and then walks quickly toward the front door.

MED. SHOT - MELANIE

enters post office.

CLOSE SHOT - POSTAL CLERK

behind cage as Melanie approaches it. He is busy filling out a form of some kind, affixing stamps to it, etc. He does not look up as she approaches.

CLOSE SHOT - MELANIE

through the bars of the cage.

                    MELANIE
               Good morning.

CLOSE SHOT - POSTAL CLERK

                    CLERK
          without looking up)
               Morning.

TWO SHOT - MELANIE AND THE CLERK

                    MELANIE
          I wonder if you could help me.

                    CLERK
               Try my best.

                    MELANIE
     I'm looking for a man named Mitchell Brenner.

                    CLERK
                    Yep.

He is still busy with his form, still does not
look up.

                    MELANIE
               Do you know him?

                    CLERK
                    Yep.

                    MELANIE
          Where does he live?

                    CLERK
          Right here. Bodega Bay.

```
                    MELANIE
              Yes, but where?


                     CLERK
            Right across the bay there.


                    MELANIE
                    Where?


It seems as if the Clerk will not answer her.
Suddenly, he leaves the window.

CLOSE SHOT - MELANIE

through the bars, exasperated.
```

I love reading through older screenplays. Decades ago, it was the screenwriter's job (when assigned to create the shooting script) to delineate every single shot in a scene, as you can see from the example of *The Birds*, which essentially meant writers had to think like directors and pay close attention to the technical aspects of a script's structure while trying to write a moving masterpiece.

What a tedious way to construct a screenplay! On one hand, the requirements of the structure took away from the creativity of writing the story (I'm thinking it must have).

On the other hand, by calling all the shots (literally), a writer took all the creativity away from the director, who was no longer wholly directing but obeying.

Directors Are More Like Writers Now

Times have changed. More and more actors are directing behind the cameras now, bringing a rich perspective to films. Writers and directors are producing, wearing more hats and being much more involved in the day-to-day production of a movie. Directors often decide how they want to shoot a scene, and scripts are written much differently, allowing the writer to use more novel-like prose and less camera specifics.

Take a look at the excerpt of *The Birds* above and notice how, at almost every line, Evan Hunter put in the type of camera shot needed every step of the way. I'm sure the director could have made those decisions just by reading the script. Frankly, I doubt Alfred Hitchcock needed any of those camera shots stated. Hitchcock did give Hunter input on how he wanted DeMaurier's novel adapted for the screen, but did he specify the camera shots? I don't know, but I doubt it.

Then go to Dailyscript.com and choose a more contemporary screenplay, like *The Shawshank Redemption*. I suggest this one because it is beautifully written, with engaging prose. So much different from *The Birds*. That's not to say old screenplays are bad and newer ones are good.

I'm just pointing out the evolution of screenwriting, allowing for both writer and director to use their creativity more fully and imaginatively. It can be worthwhile to spend some time reading through screenplays. Descriptions are brief and to the point, and always the "viewer" is being directed to only what will be shown and what must be paid attention to. Novelists can learn a lot from this.

But whether the camera shot is plainly stated or only implied in the narrative of the script, the intention of the shot is clear, and the type of shot is therefore indicated, to some extent. Whether the script reads "Close-Up—Melanie as she looks through the windshield at the town" or "We see Melanie straining to look through the window," we know this is a shot close enough to see her face, from an angle that affords us to see what she's doing.

So as you read through various screenplays, think how the camera shot is implied or stated, and why. Ask: Why is this the best shot for this segment of the scene? How does it convey the information needed as well as provide for the best emotional impact?

Later on in *The Birds*, if you recall, there are some tense moments when a whole lot of birds attack a whole lot of people. If these kinds of scenes were done as Long Shots, would they have the same suspense and emotional charge as the Close Shot in which you can see the birds pecking at skin and the characters screaming with terror etched in their faces?

What about the scene in *Psycho*—you know, the one of the knife in the shower. Picture that as a Long Shot—would that scene then have terrified viewers? I don't think so. They might have gotten up to get a refill of popcorn. And that's the last thing a writer wants her reader to do right in the middle of a tense, important, big moment in a novel.

Close Up and Personal

So, let's look at the three basic stationary "distance" shots: The Close-Up (CU or Close Shot, sometimes called a 2-Shot for two people in the shot), Medium Shot (MS, or Full Shot), and Long Shot (LS). These are the staple shots. You may also find Extreme Close-Up, Extreme Wide Shot, Very Wide Shot, Over-the-Shoulder Shot, Reverse Shot, etc. It may be superfluous to say that you want to use a Close Shot when you want to get in close and see things you can't see from far away.

The same idea applies with the Long Shot. Sometimes you want to "see" something far off and not see the details. This is a choice. As you think about the scene you plan to write, after getting clear the point of the scene and the high moment you are going to build to, no doubt you are going to have segments of your scene that will require one of these distance shots.

I'm going to start with the Close-Up since this is not only the most commonly used shot, it's also what writers tend to use predominately *instinctively*. Most scenes in most novels seem to be Close-Ups in one form or another.

It's interesting to note that the Close-Up shot is relatively new to the evolution of cinema. Originally, films were meant to replicate the experience of the theater, and you will note if you watch early silent movies that only wide shots are used, with no shots edited.

Gustav Mercado in *The Filmmaker's Eye* says that when Close-Ups came into use to home in on detail, "cinematic styles quickly departed from the exaggeration expected in theater . . . into a more naturalistic style."

Likewise, novels, over the years, have evolved from distanced narrative to implying a variety of shots from long, sweeping ones to examining details close up. Mercado states: "In terms of connecting with the audience, the CU is one of the most powerful shots used in visual storytelling, and is largely responsible for our love affair with movies."

A Close-Up Defined

Simply put, a Close-Up or Close Shot usually can include a person's head, or perhaps the heads of two people, and no more. And many scenes writers write involve conversation or action between two people. In addition, Close-Ups are used to "watch" action taking place close enough so that certain important details can be noticed.

So, use Close Shots when you want the reader to notice or pay attention to an object, a character's small action, a subtle detail like a smell, or a reaction (facial close-up).

Writing a scene using a Close-Up shot is pretty much intuitive and needs little explanation. When you watch a movie and the camera is in close (not extremely close so that only one object fills the screen and you can't notice anything else but a general Close Shot), you will notice a lot of things. The film will show you everything you can see within a few feet.

But can you imagine trying to put *everything* that can be seen into your scene? How many pages would it take to describe every piece of clothing the two characters are wearing, every item in the room, including every title of every book on the shelf, every dish on the table, every piece of furniture? Who in the world would do such a thing? No one, I hope.

How Much Is Enough? Or Too Much?

But this begs the question: How much *do* you describe in order to "set the stage" effectively?

A good question, and the answer depends on the writer's style, the genre she's writing in, and what is important to reveal. You've read books so void of close-up details you can't picture or follow what's going on. Conversely, you've no doubt read novels containing pages and pages of tedious description that seem utterly unnecessary and bog down the story.

There is a middle ground, though, and again, it points back to the point of the scene. You want to have the reader notice just enough for them to picture the scene, all the while directing them to things (items, faces, sounds, smells, etc.) that will enhance the moment, advance the plot, reveal character, and evoke emotion.

Close-Up Shots in Novels Are Evocative

For fun, I took the opening joke (about the guy who walks into the bar with the piece of asphalt) and wrote it out as a brief scene using, predominately, a Close-Up shot. I have a couple of places where I Pan or Follow my character, but the purpose of doing this is to show

how small close-up details can help make the scene come alive. Sensory details (touch, taste, sounds, sights, smells) are the most effective ways to make a scene come alive in the reader's mind, and in a Close Shot you can have your character experience things that bring intimacy to the fore.

Here's where a novelist can sometimes achieve a stronger effect than a screenwriter or filmmaker. Novelists can evoke smells and sensations in a way a movie can't. Sure, a movie can show a plate of mouthwatering pizza, and that visual can set our stomach growling. Yet, a novelist can express from the character's POV how that pizza smells and looks and makes him feel. If done well, our mouths will water as well while we read the passage, and we may even need to get up and raid the refrigerator. If you read the book *Chocolat* by Joanne Harris and you didn't go scrounging the house for something chocolate, something must be wrong with you.

So take a look at the close-up bits my character notices as he goes into the bar to get a drink. Think about how a handful of small sensory details can enhance a scene and help you get to know the character better.

The man rested a trembling hand on the burnished brass handle of the splintered wood door. He stepped into the dim room and let his eyes adjust, then walked across the room, his boots clacking on the wood planking. He heard his friend sigh and looked at his face.

The giant piece of asphalt looked haggard and parched—as if a thousand tires had just driven over his body and left him flattened and beat up. He nudged his friend as they came up to the bar and pulled a couple of crinkled bills from his pants pocket. He laid the bills on the water-stained mahogany counter and cleared his throat. He caught the bartender's attention.

The crusty old barkeep came over reeking of sweat and the sour odor of stale cigar smoke. The man's eyes caught on the long scar running under the barkeep's lip, but the glint in the old man's eye told him he'd better not mention it.

"Uh, I'll have a whiskey," he said, noticing some shady-looking characters in the recesses of the dark room. Three men pushed back their chairs and started heading his way. He gulped and wished he hadn't chosen to stop at this hole in the wall in the middle of nowhere. But he knew they couldn't have traveled much further, and the next town was nearly fifty miles away.

He should have listened to his mother's warnings not to take this highway. He'd been impatient, wanting to get to Las Vegas as quickly as possible. He needed cash, and that stolen watch was burning a hole in his pocket. He knew if he could just pawn it and play the tables, he'd get the money he needed and pay off his debt before those thugs came back.

The bartender paid him no mind, but pulled out a rag and mindlessly circled over the imbedded water stains in the wood as if he had nothing better to do.

"I said, I'll have a whiskey," the man announced in a loud voice. He glanced over at the piece of asphalt, whose eyes now showed fear. The man's mouth tightened. His pal was a chicken, always let people roll all over him. He surely wouldn't be one bit of help in a bar fight. It was time to hightail out of there before those men shook him down and discovered that watch.

He finally caught the bartender's attention. He gestured at his friend and said, "And one for the road. Make it snappy."

Close-Ups Close the Distance

Close-Ups allow writers to paint the flair into the story, which breathes life into it. Can you imagine showing every scene as if the camera was a football field away?

Yes, there are times when you don't want to show detail, and I'll get more into that later when we look at Long Shots. But I believe it would be hard to successfully write an entire novel as if watching from far away (okay, there's another challenge for those of you with too much time on your hands). Your characters would be shapes upon the landscape, and the reader wouldn't be able to tell much of what they are doing. From that far away, your reader can't hear what they're saying, or experience what they're smelling, tasting, or touching.

The distance *distances* readers—and that's a problem. Readers want to be immersed in story and character, and you can't achieve that by holding them at arm's length—or relegating them to standing a hundred yards away.

So keep this in mind as you construct your scenes. Once you have a feel for all the major kinds of camera shots and when best and how to use them, invariably there will be moments in many of your scenes in which the Close-Up shots will be key to building to and revealing your "moment."

Remember, you, the director, are in charge of showing the reader what's important. By using a Close-Up, you are saying "pay attention here!" You can add tension by revealing a clue that you don't explain until later, but if the reader is "told" to notice it, she will be curious as to why it was pointed out.

Close-Ups Are All about Details

In this scene in Linda S. Clare's novel *The Fence My Father Built*, Clare uses a Close-Up shot to have her character look at the things in the closet, then moves in with an Extreme Close-Up as she studies and reads a letter she's found.

I went to the cramped room Nova and I shared to decide on my own clothes, crammed into the closet with all sorts of boxes of Lutie's sewing supplies and who knows what else. This would be my first real social outing since we'd arrived. A few of Lutie's church ladies had stopped by—with covered dishes and a jar of last years' homemade applesauce.

I slid a boot box to one side. It fell over and its contents tumbled out. Instead of crochet hooks or balls of yarn, a pile of papers and old photos lay at my feet. On a yellowed photo the likeness of Joseph Pond stared up at me.

He stood on a rise overlooking the creek. Shadows cut across the landscape and my father's profile.

I picked up the snapshot and smoothed it, running my fingers across his face. I sat on the edge of the bed and tried to pray for the first time since I could remember. I felt awkward and clumsy but I asked for guidance anyway. Before I could stop it, a tear splashed on the print. I wiped it away and wished I'd come here while he was still alive.

This was what was left of my father: old pictures, clippings, cocktail napkins scrawled with drawings and a letter, on lined paper, written in a strong upright hand.

My Dear Daughter, Muriel, the letter began. What followed was a heartbreaking admission of parental failure, but also an unbendable faith. My father admitted he was a problem drinker and hadn't been capable of raising his only offspring. One line jumped out and pricked my heart: The good Lord has been good to this old sinner, it said, and I'd die a happy man if I knew you'd joined the fold of our Lord Jesus.

I still wasn't sure I could enter into his beliefs. "I want to believe," I said out loud, "but I'm so confused. I just don't see how God can help me in my situation." I carefully folded the letter and placed it in my wallet, for safekeeping. I gently laid the other things back into the box and slid it back where I'd found it. I wondered if Aunt Lutie had planted it there for me to find.

Can you see how Clare used those camera shots for close-up detail? The details writers bring to the fore should give insight into the characters and move the plot forward. By being deliberate in the choice of camera shots and using them in a natural, unforced way—mimicking the way we move through life and see and interact with our world—writers can tell a powerful, effective story. And getting "up close and personal" is the best way to get there.

Close-Ups Enhance Theme

Think about an Extreme Close-Up. When you are watching a movie and the camera "blows up" some detail you would normally not see unless you were within inches of it, you are forced to look at it, and it alone. You are, in effect, being told to pay specific attention, even if you are not told why. This technique is powerful in film, and often is used in a symbolic manner. How better to bring out a theme or motif than by using this technique?

In David Lynch's film *Blue Velvet* (1986), after showing a montage of an idyllic small-town American landscape, the sequence ends with an Extreme Close-Up of beetles crawling under a beautifully manicured lawn. The symbolism would be hard to miss: under the pristine outer appearance of sublime American life and order, there are creepy crawly things tearing up the earth and creating havoc. What a powerful way to imply there is something ugly simmering (or crawling) beneath the surface!

Writers can apply this technique without much difficulty. A POV character in a scene can shift her attention during or after a peak moment to notice something around her. In that flash of moment, she can either see the connection between her present circumstance or she can just be riveted without knowing why.

Either way, by bringing the detail up extremely close, the reader is hit with the significance (in filmmaking known as the Hitchcock Rule—the size of the image in the frame implying how important it is to the story). And if a novel is using a repetitive motif or thematic element such as something in nature, bringing this up close from time to time will powerfully punch home the theme. A common use of the Extreme Close-Up is to draw attention to a detail that is seemingly unimportant but has weighty significance later on.

So now, with the Close-Up shot in your writer's toolbox, let's move on.

Chapter 4

A Bigger Perspective

Full Shot for Full Effect

There are an array of shots that fall between a Close-Up and a Long Shot, and they might be called a Full Shot, Medium Shot, Medium Long Shot, Figure Shot, or Complete View—but you probably get the idea. I'm going to simplify these in order to generalize their usage for a novelist's purpose.

A Full Shot will show full figures or at least from the waist up (depending on the lens and type of Medium Shot). These shots showcase body language, and include facial nuances. They convey the dynamics of relationship through placement of characters in relation to one another and to the space/setting around them.

A Full Shot may cover a conversation until an important point is being reached, and then either the Zoom or Close-Up will come into play—or a Pull Back to a Long Shot, to reveal a bigger picture. After the climactic moment, a return to the Full Shot might be utilized.

If you have a fight scene with two men hitting and struggling, you may not want the camera in so close you only see the faces. You want the reader to see those arms swinging and legs kicking. Yet, you don't want to be so far away you can't hear the moans of pain or see the blood flying when the bad guy gets his nose broken by a hard punch.

Think about what you might see in a Full Shot. What someone is wearing, for example. If the guy sees his date walk in, he's going to look her over, and you would use a Full Shot to show what he's seeing.

Taking in a Whole Group

The Medium Shot also works best when you want to get in close to a small group of people.

Let's say you have your characters at a party, or they're a family sitting at the dinner table, eating and talking. You may get in close from time to time when you need to show those small details the Medium Shot won't notice (like when Junior slips Max the dog situated under the table the broccoli he doesn't want to eat), but to get everyone "in the picture" as the scene plays out, you'll want a Medium Shot for the most part.

In Suzanne Collins's runaway best seller *The Hunger Games*, we find her heroine, Katniss, high up in a tree, positioned safely from the other "tributes" below who want to kill her. Earlier, she found a way to saw through most of a branch on which a large nest of deadly tracker jackers sits. Her aim? To dump them on her enemies below. Although the novel is told in first person, she shifts her "inner" camera POV to a Medium Shot as she (and the reader) watches what happens.

. . . And just as the knife cuts through, I shove the end of the branch as far away from me as I can. It crashes down through the lower branches, snagging temporarily on a few but then twisting free until it smashes with a thud on the ground. The nest bursts open like an egg, and a furious swarm of tracker jackers takes to the air . . .

It's mayhem. The Careers have woken to a full-scale tracker jacker attack. Peeta and a few others have the sense to drop everything and bolt. I can hear cries of "To the lake! To the lake!" and know they hope to evade the wasps by taking to the water. It must be close if they think they can outdistance the furious insects. Glimmer and another girl, the one from district 4, are not so lucky. They receive multiple stings before they're even out of my view. Glimmer appears to go completely mad, shrieking and trying to bat the wasps off with her bow, which is pointless. She calls to the others for help but, of course, no one returns. . . . I watch Glimmer fall, twitch hysterically around on the ground for a few minutes, and then go still.

The nest is nothing but an empty shell. The wasps have vanished in pursuit of the others.

Notice what details Katniss can and can't see with this Medium Shot. She's close enough to watch the teens get stung, and hear what they say, as well as their cries of pain. She can see Glimmer try to use her bow to swat at the jackers. Katniss is close to danger, and not out of danger at all, yet she's far enough away to "document" what goes on below her. And no, she doesn't get away unscathed, for she gets stung as the nest begins to fall.

What follows shifts to more of a series of Close Shots and internal thinking as she makes her way out of her perch, finally safely able to get away, and starts to feel the effects of the poisonous venom in her system. The brief but necessary Medium Shot accomplished what Collins aimed to do—present the real action from a viewpoint that would give the strongest effect and stay true to her POV character's point of view.

Choose Believable Circumstances

And that's something to consider. Circumstances may often dictate which camera shot is used. Katniss, from her high vantage point, could not see close-up details.

Sure, it might have been more intense if the reader could have gotten up close to the Careers (those who spend their lives preparing to participate in the Hunger Games) and nearly tasted their fear, but it wouldn't be feasible or believable. Katniss is high up in a tree, and the scene is observed through her eyes. Unless she had binoculars, she would not be able to see such detail.

If it's crucial your character has to notice something that requires an Extreme Close-Up, such as a medical examiner finding a sliver of glass under a homicide victim's fingernail, make sure you provide a scene in which it's believable for her to do so.

Full Shots Are Still Close

In Leif Enger's beautiful novel *Peace like a River*, eleven-year-old Reuben Land describes what happens in the bedroom he shares with his older brother, Davy. It's late and the brothers are in bed, but trouble is brewing and has been for a while. Reuben startles at the sound of the floorboards creaking downstairs and trembles as he hears someone approaching their room.

He realizes he's waited too long to wake his brother. And then . . .

The steps came forward. They stopped at my door. I felt, more than heard, someone's hand upon the knob.

Then Davy spoke from beside me—"Switch on the light"— his voice so soft he might've been talking in his sleep. But he wasn't. He was talking to whoever stood incorporeal in the doorway. "Switch it *on*," he commanded, and next thing we were all of us brightsoaked and blinking: me beneath my quilt, and Israel Finch standing in the door with a baseball bat in one hand and the other still on the switch, and poor stupid Tommy all asquint behind his shoulder. Davy was sitting up in bed in his T-shirt, hair askew. Somehow he was holding the little Winchester he'd carried in the timber that afternoon. And holding it comfortably: elbows at rest on his knees, his cheek against the stock, as if to plink tin cans off fence posts.

It is fair to say that Israel had no chance. I'm not saying he deserved one. He stood in the door with his pathetic club like primal man squinting at extinction. How confused he looked, how pinkeyed and sweaty! Then he lifted the bat, the knothead, and Davy fired, and Israel went backward into Tommy Basca, and Davy levered up a second round and fired again. . . .

The round made a bright black raindrop above and between his two eyebrows . . . Swede came flying from her room. She saw, besides Finch, Tommy Basca on his stomach with hands aquiver toward the door, and Davy stepping up behind him. . . . Tommy clawed the floor, bawling incomprehensibly, and his eyes rolled, and there was genuine terror inside his voice, and I knew with certainty he was seeing all the devils waiting for him . . . Standing above him, Davy levered up a third cartridge.

I ought've looked away, but I couldn't.

He lowered the barrel to the base of Tommy Basca's skull. For an instant my brother seemed very small—like a stranger seen at a clear distance. He showed no tremor. He fired. Tommy relaxed.

Reuben is close enough to see both his brother and the two teens intent on harm. Close enough to catch the significant bits of action: the way Davy's sitting with the gun and his quiet sleep-walking-sounding voice, the confusion in Israel's eyes and his sweat, Tommy squinting, the blood appearing on his forehead from the bullet wound, his eyes rolling. All this is perfectly shown with a Medium Shot.

Enger is able to get in all the important details and nuances to make the scene alive, cinematic. Note, though, how well he colors the action through his protagonist's eyes, showing what an eleven-year-old boy would notice in particular—like the words and noises uttered and the looks on the boys' faces. This altercation surely is the high moment of this scene, and the way Enger almost pauses with the line "for an instant my brother seemed very small—like a stranger seen at a distance" places importance on this brief moment, in a sense blowing it up to be the pivotal few seconds of not only the scene but of perhaps the entire novel.

Interesting how Reuben, although fairly close to his brother, now sees him *as if* in a Long Shot, which Enger uses *as metaphor*. For, now, this brother of his is like a stranger he can barely make out, acting in ways never imagined, shooting holes into not just these boys and the lives of Reuben's entire family but tearing into Reuben's almost worshipful adoration of Davy. Beautifully done.

Too Far to Really Tell

Long Shots in novels are not often used. Why? Well, when you are a half mile away from something, you really can't see all that much. But that is exactly why and when you want to use this particular shot. We looked at the use of Long Shots for Establishing Shots, but they can be used in other ways. For filmmakers, Long Shots can be used to emphasize a character and the space around her, and for a novelist, they can turn attention to the setting. They can be used to limit the emotional involvement of the audience—they distance the viewer/reader from what is happening.

Anytime you want to create a mystery or show something fuzzy, not clearly seen or defined, a Long Shot can be the right choice of camera angle. Something observed can be mistaken or misinterpreted, a voice yelled can go unheard, a danger coming up over the horizon can be unnamable and thus more terrifying. A tornado or hurricane roiling in the distance can build tension. Knowing what *may* be coming or what *may* be happening can add great microtension to a novel. So you might do well to look for opportunities in your story to use a Long Shot.

Then there are the epic or panorama views you want the reader to see and feel. Whether showing a glorious morning bursting upon the beach after a terrific storm or a scene like the one in *Gone with the Wind*, in which the whole of Atlanta is burning and Rhett and Scarlett are fleeing in the wagon, nothing beats a Long Shot for effect. (Well, actually that was a studio lot in Culver City, and it was agreed they'd shoot this scene first to get rid of some old sets to make way to build the new ones needed of the plantations and city streets for the rest of the movie—just to throw in a bit of movie trivia here.)

Action-packed movies are a blend of Close-Ups and Long Shots (and just about every moving shot too). The camera narrows in on the faces of the actors as they tensely rig the bomb to blow, then cuts to the Extreme Long Shot to show the massive explosion. Disaster movies have Long Shots galore, and if you are writing an action-suspense novel you'll want a lot of Long Shots in your scenes—shown from the POV characters' eyes. Find ways to position your characters so they can see the "big picture" of what is happening around them.

Long Shots Can Delay Resolution and Add Tension

Take a look at the ending of suspense writer Terry Blackstock's first scene in her novel *Predator*. The short chapter opens in the mire of tragedy. Krista is at hope's end. Her younger teenage sister, Ella, has been missing for two weeks now, and the news she has dreaded hearing comes to her: the police have found the body of a girl in the woods. They take Krista to the crime scene to see if she can identify the brutally murdered and partially buried body—a powerful, riveting opening to the book. But watch how Blackstock uses the camera effectively to build tension. She doesn't just take her protagonist straight to the body, close up and personal. Instead, she draws out the moment with a Long Shot.

> He [the officer] took her arm and walked her toward the investigators. When she reached them, she realized the body was another twenty-five yards beyond them. "You can't go any closer," the lieutenant said in a soft voice, "There could be footprints or trace evidence." . . .
>
> Nausea rose, but she stood paralyzed, staring toward the mound of dirt where the girl lay. She couldn't see a thing. Not what she was wearing or the color of her hair . . .

Krista waited, willing back the numbness, certain she wouldn't recognize the girl. As the first raindrops fell, a man in a medical examiner's jacket took in a gurney, and Krista watched as they pulled the body from its shallow tomb. She saw the pink-striped shirt that Ella was wearing that last day. Blond hair matted with blood and earth.

Her knees went weak, turned to rubber. She dropped and hit the ground. At once, a crowd of police surrounded her, asking if she was okay. She blinked and sat up, let them pull her back to her feet.

Ella!

She heard footsteps pounding the dirt.

"Aw, no! No! It can't be her!" Her father's voice, raspy and heart-wrenching, wailed out over the crowd. She wanted to go to him, comfort him, but it was as though her hands were bound to her sides and her legs wouldn't move.

As they brought the girl closer, Krista saw the bloody, bruised face. Ella's face.

The search was over. Her sister was dead.

By Blackstock having her character first unable to see a thing, only a mound of dirt, she stretches out the tension for the reader. She has to wait (and so does the reader) agonizing moments until the body is pulled out and she can make out the shirt and the hair—not the face, because she's not close enough—but seeing the shirt is conclusive enough for her.

You Can Pick Up Facial Expressions and Gestures

Here's another wonderful example of a Long Shot—a great choice by author Philippa Gregory in her best seller *The Other Boleyn Girl*. Notice the details her character, young Mary, can see from where she stands—and what she can't see. It's the perfect opening shot to give a sense of the scope of the crowd and the event taking place, yet close enough for Mary to note the subtle actions and expressions of those she is watching.

I could hear a roll of muffled drums. But I could see nothing but the lacing on the bodice of the lady standing in front of me, blocking my view of the scaffold. . . .

By stepping to one side a little and craning my neck, I could see the condemned man, accompanied by his priest, walk slowly from the Tower toward the green where the wooden platform was waiting, the block of wood placed center stage, the executioner dressed all ready for work in his shirtsleeves with a black hood over his head. It looked more like a masque than a real event, and I watched it as if it were a court entertainment. The king, seated on his throne, looked distracted, as if he was running through his speech of forgiveness in his head. Behind him stood my husband of one year, William Carey, my brother, George, and my father, Sir Thomas Boleyn, all looking grave. I wriggled my toes inside my silk slippers and wished the king would hurry up and grant clemency so that we could all go to breakfast. I was only thirteen years old. I was always hungry.

The Duke of Buckinghamshire, far away on the scaffold, put off his thick coat. He was close enough kin for me to call him uncle. . . .

Uncle Stafford came to the front of the stage to say his final words. I was too far from him to hear, and in any case I was watching the king, waiting for his cue to step forward and offer the royal pardon. The man standing on the scaffold, in the sunlight of the early morning, had been the king's partner at tennis, his rival on the jousting field, his friend at a hundred bouts of drinking and gambling; they had been comrades since the king was a boy. The king was teaching him a lesson . . . and then he would forgive him and we could all go to breakfast.

Mary can tell by the king's expression that he seems distracted—that's something she wouldn't be able to tell from too far away. Yet she is not close enough to hear the words being said by her uncle.

No doubt, at an occasion such as this, she would not be able to get too close, and Gregory's use of the Long Shot invites more emotional punch by having Mary not able to discern clearly that the outcome of this affair will turn out much differently than she expected.

Long Shots Make Great High Moment Shots

Long Shots "blow up" a scene, make it huge and powerful. They can also add subtle poignancy when the hero rides off into the sunset (or whatever that equates to in your book and genre). Long Shots can say "This is the result of what just happened." That moment often ranks as a high moment in a scene, and even for the entire novel.

Sometimes filmmakers will use an Extreme Long Shot to emphasize the vastness of location, usually following a Close-Up, indicating the character has just seen or realized something important, and those two shots in sequence add tension. Novelists can do the same in their scenes.

Do you recall how the movie *Casablanca* ends? Rick and Louis walk together (Two Shot) and then head off across the Tarmac (Follows), which shifts the scene into a Long Shot. Instead of the camera moving, the actors move farther and farther away. Can you think of a better shot to go with Bogart's famous line: "Louis, I think this is the beginning of a beautiful friendship"? I can't. The Long Shot lingers long in the mind—a great tool to put in your cinematic toolbox.

Chapter 5

Slip in a Slide Show

Montages for Powerful Imagery

A montage comprises a series of shots that are separate events, not connected in time (that's a Series of Shots and we'll look at that next). They move chronologically forward and they might cover just a few minutes or possibly years. But the purpose of a Montage Shot is to speed time up by "summarizing" what happens over a period of time regarding something specific.

If you just want your next scene in your novel to take place three months after the scene preceding it, you can just state that somewhere in the first few lines or in a subheading.

Movies will jump ahead like that as well, making it clear in the opening moments that some amount of time has passed. But there are times when you want to show a progression of incidents, a gradual change that comes, specific to the plot and serving the needs of the plot.

Montages are very common in contemporary movies, especially in chick flicks. They can be used for a variety of reasons, but the main one I've noticed is to imply a passage of time. Often about two-thirds through a movie a great song (usually the movie's hit song) will play while a montage takes place—one visual after another showing how some days or weeks have gone by, marked by the "progression" of what's being shown.

Using Steps to Skip the Steps

Aside from the classic *Rocky* (1976, and some if not all of the other *Rocky* movies), with its montage of training shots, two movies come to mind, and both are centered on dancing: *Footloose* and *Strictly Ballroom*. I happen to love movies with dance scenes (prefer them over fighting ones), and the montage scenes in these two movies are classic. In fact, I can think of two montage dance scenes in *Strictly Ballroom*. Maybe there are even more. But they are a great tool to use when you want to speed up time and events and move ahead to the next big, important event in the story.

In *Footloose*, Kevin Bacon's character, Ren McCormack, has told his two friends he's going to take them to a dance despite their being forbidden to go. Ariel is a natural, but Willard can't dance—so Ren says he'll teach him. What follows is a montage of shots showing a progression of Willard going from having two left feet to actually being able to bust some impressive moves. In the movie, the sequence only lasts as long as Denice Williams can sing "Let's Hear It for the Boy." We get the feeling that hours have passed by the time it's over, and that's the point. Who wants to watch hours of someone learning to dance? No one. So this is a nifty way of fast-forwarding time.

The same exact thing is done in *Strictly Ballroom*. Tryouts are held in the search for a new partner for Scott Hastings—ballroom dance phenomenon. A montage of clips plays showing a string of really bad dancers on the screen, implying days are going by with no success to find the ideal partner for Scott. In another part of the movie, we watch Scott and Francesca practice for the big ballroom competition (The Pan-Pacific Grand Prix Dancing Championship) to Cyndi Lauper singing "Time after Time." Fran is a pathetic frumpy beginner, but by the end of the sequence she's actually starting to look pretty darn good. By the end of the movie, she's turned from ugly duckling into Cinderella, perfect for this fairy-tale story.

You can probably think of a number of movies that use a montage of scenes, and since they're so popular it begs the question: How can novelists utilize this camera technique effectively to accomplish the same thing—moving time along and leaving the reader with a particular emotional resonance? Okay, I do have to mention before moving on the great montage scene in *Robin Hood: Prince of Thieves* (1991) in which Kevin Costner as Robin Hood is gearing up with weapons and other accoutrements for war while a rousing song plays in the background.

And don't forget Forrest Gump running back and forth across the US for three years, two months, and fourteen days to Jackson Browne singing "Running on Empty." And then, of course, there's *The Karate Kid*, *Ghostbusters*, *Scarface*, *The Naked Gun*, *Fight Club*, *Ferris Bueller's Day Off* . . .

Your Life Flashing before Your Eyes

Think about a character in a novel—let's say a mother sitting in church waiting for her daughter to come down the aisle in her beautiful white wedding gown. This is a key moment in this mother's life. All the years she spent raising her daughter have brought them both to this moment. Perhaps she's regretted the way she raised her, feeling she's been a failure as a mother. Maybe she's suffering from empty nest syndrome. Whatever this character is feeling at this key moment in her life in the story can be heightened by the use of a montage scene.

As the daughter begins her long walk toward her anxious husband-to-be, the mother may think back to her daughter as an infant. Then she might recall her first baby steps, then holding her hand as she walked her to her first day at kindergarten. Then there was the time she starred in the sixth-grade musical, and learned how to drive a car (wasn't that a near-disaster!), and then high school graduation, her senior prom, her first date. Think how many things often flash through your mind when reminded of an important time or person in your life. What happens when you run into someone you haven't seen in ten years? What if that person was your first love—or your violent ex-spouse?

Memories Appear Often to Us as Montages

Your characters can and should think the way humans normally do, and often we experience a montage of memories. And they don't have to be memories; they can be "what ifs." Thoughts of what might happen *if* I make this choice. Your character can envision all the possibilities of an action. What about a mother whose child has been kidnapped, as we saw in the novel *Predator*? Can you picture a montage of thoughts going through her head—the worst possible thoughts she doesn't want to consider?

So whether you want to fast-forward time in your novel, or flip through the memories of the past, or have a character consider all the "what ifs," using a montage technique may serve your story best.

Speeding Up Time

Take a look at this excerpt from the movie *The Conspiracy Theory*. In just a short bit of time and with just a few key montage images, we get a very good picture of this paranoid man named Jerry. Mel Gibson plays this role exceptionally well, demonstrating the manic, erratic behavior that makes the viewer wonder just how nuts Jerry really is. Of course, as the plot unfolds, we realize why Jerry is so messed up. In this very early scene, the screenwriter is able to pack in a lot of information by utilizing this camera shot.

THE CONSPIRACY THEORY

Screenplay by Brian Helgeland, 1996
Directed by Richard Donner

INT. APARTMENT 202 - JERRY'S BEDROOM - NIGHT

Carrying a bowl of tapioca, Jerry enters. More files, a manual typewriter. On the wall, an American flag alongside a poster of John Lennon reading: "Assassinated 12/8/80."

He strides to his desk and a ...

PUBLISHING MONTAGE BEGINS

Jerry scans a *New York Times* spread on a drafting table. He circles headlines, names, and dates. Does the same with the *San Francisco Chronicle*, *Le Monde*, *Time*, the *Economist*, and *Popular Mechanics*. He enters raw data on 3x5 cards: space shuttle launched, base closings, escape from mental hospital, and especially the obituaries. Specifically: "Industrialist Ernest Hariman Drowns."

Jerry flips through hundreds of cards on big Rolodexes as he cross-references data. Jerry pulls cards, lines them up. The first connection: the dates of six Space Shuttle launches and six earthquakes all coinciding. Jerry lets out a low whistle. Never too jaded to be shocked.

Jerry types the text of an article, crosses out mistakes. He hand-cranks copies off an old drum mimeograph. The hand-drawn logo: lips whispering into an ear. The title: "Conspiracy Theory."

Jerry writes out five labels. Addresses from across America. Jerry slaps the labels on the newsletters.

EXT. STREET

The sun comes up.

Jerry drops the newsletters into a mailbox. He starts across the street, then stops, looks back with dread. He steps back over, checks the slot. Everything went down. Jerry starts away, then stops again. As he looks back...

DISSOLVE TO:

EXT. JUSTICE DEPARTMENT - NYC OFFICES - DAY

Can you think how you might translate this montage into a novel's scene? Instead of writing pages and pages showing everything Jerry did hour after hour until the sun came up, you could have Jerry, bleary-eyed but running on high-octane paranoia, looking around his bedroom before heading out to mail his meager five newsletters to his subscribers. All these moments could flash through his mind as he scans his stacks of papers and notes. Or you could play out his actions, with one line for each image, compiling item after item until it fills the page, noting how the sun starts coming up by the time he's done.

There is no right way to do a montage sequence in a novel. You just want to give that sense of a succession of thoughts or actions compressed in a period of time.

For speeding up the passage of time, nothing beats a Montage. And probably no film shows an overview of earth's history as quickly and chaotically as the brief segment of montage shots in the movie *Adaptation* by Charlie Kaufman (2000):

```
MONTAGE

This   sequence   shows   the   entire   history   of
mankind   from  a  world  sparsely  populated  with
primitive      hunter-gatherers      to      today's
overcrowded  technological  society.  We  see  the
history   of   architecture,   war,   religion,
commerce.  We  see  murder  and  procreation.  We  see
man  interacting  with  his  environment:  farming,
eating  meat,  admiring  a  view.  We  see  old  age
and   birth.   We   see   it   again   and   again   at
dizzying  speed.  We  see  Laroche  as  a  child  alone
with   his  turtles.   We   see   Orlean   as   a   child
alone   with   her   diary.   We   see   Alice   serving
food,  smiling  at  customers.  We  finish  on  sad
Kaufman  getting  into  his  car  and  leaving  the
Santa  Barbara  Orchid  Show.  The  entire  sequence
takes  two  minutes.
```

Montages as Imagery

Here's an excerpt from a fantasy book by Roger Zelazny called *The Guns of Avalon*, the second book of the five-book Amber series—a favorite of mine. In Zelazny's world, the princes and princesses of Amber, the true world, can create and move through fabricated (shadow) worlds that are only reflections and variations of the true Amber. In order to move through one world to another, these characters have to alter the world they are in one piece at a time by willing the change. They see in their minds what they want to shift, and the world is effected in response. Zelazny paints a wild canvas of imagery that literally goes on for pages, taking the reader on something akin to a video-game experience as his protagonist, Corwin, shifts his world around him to get to the one he strives for.

I turned and continued southward, confirmed in my desire to succeed. Amber I do not forget . . .

The sun became a dazzling, bright blister above my head and the winds began to scream about me. The sky grew more and more yellow and glaring as I rode, until it was as if a desert stretched from horizon to horizon overhead. The hills grew rockier as I descended toward the lowlands . . .

Then long shadows, the dying of the wind, stillness . . . Only the click of hoof on rock and the sounds of breathing . . . Now a rippling, glassy curtain to my right as the rain advances . . . Blue fracture lines within the clouds . . . The temperature plummeting, our pace steady, the world a monochromatic backdrop now . . .

Gonging thunder, flashing white, the curtain flaring toward us now . . . two hundred meters . . . One fifty . . . Enough!

It's bottommost edge plowing, furrowing, frothing . . . The moist smell of the earth . . . Star's whinny . . . A burst of speed.

Small rivulets of water creeping outward, sinking, staining the ground . . . Now bubbling muddily, now trickling . . . Now a steady flow . . .

And on it goes. But the effect of the endless short images creates just the feel Zelazny is going for, and using a Montage camera technique is the best way to do this.

Montage Imagery to Condense a Story

Imagery montage can also be used to tell a story in a short period of time. Flashes of key moments in an event can work powerfully to trigger emotional response.

Use as model for inter this flashbacks →

Take a look at this intense and moving scene in the movie *K-Pax* (2001). The screenwriters, Gene Brewer and Charles Leavitt, could have just had the sheriff sitting with Dr. Mark Powell and telling him the gruesome story of Robert Porter coming home after work and finding a man in his house who had just raped and murdered his wife and daughter. How powerful would that have been on a scale of one to ten? Maybe a zero.

Instead they create a Montage of shots with Powell picturing the play of horrific events as the sheriff walks him through the house. The result is a stunning, heartbreaking tale that ends with Powell finally understanding everything he has sought to learn through the entire movie. It is *the* key scene of the film, and so the writers wisely chose the best type of camera shot for the most potent effect.

                              SHERIFF
          Had   detectives   come   from   Albuquerque
          try   an'   piece   this   one   together.
          Accordin' to the official story . . .
          Porter   was   at   work   . . .when   this
          drifter, a Daryl Walker, came by the
          house. Two-time parolee, lookin' for
          trouble. Know what I'm sayin'? Started
          out   as   a   robbery.   Wife   and   daughter
          were out back . . .

          CLOSER ON POWELL . . . he gazes out past the
          hinges of what once was a back door. He hears
          Prot's VOICE calling . . . "Becky? Sarah?"

          AND HE FLASHES ON:

          PROT'S FACE. But it is now ROBERT POERTER'S
          FACE. A happy, tired humanity on it as he gets
          out of his truck, overalls stained after a hard
          day's work. He waits for his daughter to run
          out of the house and into his arms. Waits . . .

          But he is met with an eerie silence. Perplexed,
          he heads up the stone path and into the HOUSE.

SHERIFF (V.O.)
What we gather . . . from forensics
and all, was that this Walker
brought both women back in the
house at gunpoint.

FOLLOWING PORTER—his boots trudge up the
stairs, face growing worried at the silence.

PORTER
Becca . . . Saree?

His breathing becomes quicker, panicked, as he
moves down the narrow hallway . . . sees a doll
on the floor . . . an overturned watering can
. . . he comes to the bedroom . . .

AS WE COME BACK TO:
POWELL'S EYES, wide, shaken, listening to the
sheriff. . .

SHERIFF (V.O.)
Raped the wife. Then shot them both.

POWELL FLASHES ON:

THE BEDROOM . . . blood everywhere . . . hands
tied to bedposts . . . naked legs splayed . . .
bare feet dangling over the sides of a bed.

ON PORTER . . . witnessing this, eyes frozen.
He wears the look of a man whose universe has,
in one instant, shattered. And left him in the
airless blackness of space. From deep within
him comes a choking sound . . .

SHERIFF (V.O.)
Porter must've come home, found
Walker still here . . .

Porter staggers back into the hallway—to see
WALKER, who, scared, takes out a gun. Dazed,
but with an animal-like reflex, Porter knocks

it out of his hand. They struggle for the gun, like two grunting beasts, until Porter . . . with an inhuman strength, grabs Walker's wrist and pins him to the wall. Then raises his other fist . . . a savage look coming into his eyes. A look built up over a lifetime of meekness.

AND WE STAY ON PORTER'S FACE as, with final savagery, he sends the side of his fist into Walker's neck . . .

               SHERIFF (V.O.)
   And then knocked the son'n'bitch like an Angus steer . . .

                                 BACK TO:
POWELL as he closes his eyes.

                 POWELL
   God almighty . . .

                SHERIFF
   Snapped a grown man's neck like it was a twig.(looks tightly at Powell)Can't say I wouldn't've done the same.

The Sheriff puts his hat on, walks out, down the rubble of back steps. Powell follows him.

EXT. PORTER HOUSE - OUT BACK - DAY

As the sheriff continues on, toward the trees, Powell lingers a moment to view a withered vegetable garden. He approaches it, astonished . . . to see . . .

The remains of a LAWN SPRINKLER somehow saved from fire. It sits there in the grip of weeds, attached to a blackened hose. Along with the scorched handles of what's left of a child's jump rope. And as Powell stares at it . . .

AN IMAGE FLASHES ACROSS HIS EYES:

A beautiful young woman, long black hair
shining in the sun . . . and a little girl.
They jump rope barefoot, innocently, happily,
in the spray of the water.

THEN ANOTHER IMAGE:

Dusk. Robert Porter, staggering out of the
house. He kneels down, trying to wash the blood
off his hands in the sprinkler, sees the jump
rope . . .

As Powell blinks the images from his mind . . .

A FINAL ONE COMES TO HIM:

NIGHT . . . Porter stands on the bank of a
rushing RIVER. He stares, as if into nothing.
Overalls spattered with the dried blood of both
man and slaughtered cows. With one hand . . .
he rips off the straps, lets the overalls fall
off him. With the other hand, he tears the
shirt off his chest. Naked now . . . devoid of
any human expression . . . he drops into the
water . . . letting it carry him away . . .

                  SHERIFF (V.O.)
  We found his clothes here. Probably
  where he jumped in . . .

EXT. RIVER - DAY

  Powell stares into the rushing white water.
  He and the sheriff standing, carefully, on
  the bank.

Novelists can achieve a similar effect, using brief flashbacks *while*
keeping the POV character in the present action. The reason backstory

and flashbacks are often discouraged is they stop the present action and take the reader out of the current story. But when done like this, they only enhance the present moment, the montage of images each short and emotionally packed to deliver a punch to the gut.

Is there a place in your novel where your character learns something startling that happened in the past? Consider using the Montage sequence for impact.

Montages to Imply State of Mind

Here's a brief but effective use of Montage in Meg Moseley's book *When Sparrows Fall*. What better way to convey the disjointed sense of time and events as her character Miranda is waking up in a hospital after a serious accident?

Miranda struggled out of a groggy sleep and recalled a man standing beside her bed. "It's all right," the stranger had said. "I'll take care of the kids."

No, not quite a stranger. Jack. Unless she'd dreamed him.

What was he doing in her bedroom?

She fingered the bedding. It was wrong. A fuzzy blanket instead of her soft quilt and smooth sheets. And her hand hurt.

Everything hurt.

She fought to open her eyes. Her head drummed with a dull ache that was pierced by daggers when she made the slightest movement. She turned anyway and saw closed blinds on an unfamiliar wall. Everything kept spinning and thumping.

She closed her eyes. The throbbing continued. Desperate to know where she was, she turned slowly in the other direction before she opened her eyes again.

A pale blue curtain hung from the ceiling. A room divider.

A hospital room. That antiseptic smell. That quiet bustling.

Past hours came back in bits and pieces. Intense pain encasing her chest, her shoulder. Ice packs, bandages, IV lines.

A move from one room to another. A nurse who hummed and a roommate who snored.

A doctor who pried her eyelids open and mumbled at her.

Something rustled. The room divider swayed. A thin woman in a green shirt loomed over the bed, out of focus, and fiddled with the IV bag.

"You awake, hon?"

"I . . . I think so."

The nurse smiled. "Maybe not, then. Do you remember what happened?"

Miranda lay still, trying to sort memory from nightmare, and nightmare from dream. "I fell?"

"You sure did. You've had a concussion, not to mention a collapsed lung and some broken ribs and a separated shoulder. Pretty impressive road rash, too. Did you know that?"

Moseley uses short, clipped phrases to help give the feel of a glimpse or impression of memory. Miranda can't recall the details, but has faint recollections of the ice packs, the move to another room, a nurse who hummed, a roommate who snored. Moseley could have used full sentences and had her recall all these things in more of a continuous flashback but instead chose to use a Montage to give the feel she wanted in this scene.

Keep this camera shot in mind when you want quick and fleeting images going through a character's head.

Montages are powerful camera shots, and now that you see the ways they can be used to flip through memories, "what ifs," and confused thoughts, I hope you'll use this cinematic tool to supercharge your writing.

Chapter 6

Series of Shots for Quick Action

Another commonly used camera directive is a Series of Shots. Some think a Series of Shots is the same thing as a Montage, but it's quite different. A Series of Shots is just that—a series of consecutive shots but in immediacy. This camera technique is used mostly for fast action.

You might have a high-action scene in your novel, and your Series of Shots could look like this:

1. Car screeches around a tight curve on the treacherous mountain road

2. Driver reaches over and tries to strangle the woman passenger sitting next to him

3. Passenger door flings open and the woman jumps out of the car

4. Driver quickly wrenches the wheel to avoid going off the cliff

5. Woman tumbles down the hill

6. Car skids out, careens into the hillside, and explodes

When writing fast-action or high-suspense moments, writers are encouraged to use short words, sentences, and paragraphs. Take a look at some action-thrillers and see how great writers do this. Writing in this clipped style gives a sense of urgency and makes time move quickly. The pacing feel fast. Superfluous words are cut; lines of explanation or backstory are omitted. Every word counts.

A Lot Happens in a Short Period of Time

In one of my favorite novels, *Shibumi*, by Trevanian, we see a terrifically tense scene deftly woven with the use of a Series of Shots camera technique. Hel finds himself trapped in an underground cavern where he and his close friend Le Cagot were spelunking. The bad guys have not only killed his friend but sealed the only exit out of the cave. Hel's only option is to venture madly into the underground river cutting through the "Wine Cellar" in the hopes it will suck him down and through to freedom outside the mountain.

But he has no idea if any navigable wide-enough egress exists. With his faceplate now cracked and his jaw broken from a fall, his last flare sputters out, throwing him into darkness that closes in on his mind "with a crushing weight."

Pay attention to how Trevanian uses this series of quick images, speeding up at the end of the passage as Hel's desperation grows and his air diminishes.

Nothing in the world would be easier than to accept death with dignity, with *shibumi*. . . .

He wedged the rubberized flashlight between two outcroppings of aragonite, and using its beam attached the mask to the air tank, grunting with pain as he tightened the connections with his flayed fingers. After carefully threading the straps over his bruised shoulder, he opened the inflow valve, then dipped up a little spit water to clear the faceplate of breath mist. The pressure of the mask against his broken jaw was painful, but he could manage it. . . .

He took a deep breath and braced his nerves, remembering how that current had snatched away the dye packets so quickly that the eye could not follow them.

Almost leisurely, his body floated toward the bottom of the sump pit. That was his last clear image.

The current gripped him, and he shot into the pipe. His foot hit something; the leg crumpled, the knee striking his chest; he was spinning; the flashlight was gone; he took a blow on the spine, another on the hip.

And suddenly he was lodged behind a choke stone, and the water was roaring past him, tearing at him. The mask twisted, and the faceplate blew out, the broken pieces cutting his leg as they flashed past. He had been holding his breath from fear for several seconds, and the need for air was pounding in his temples. Water rushed over his face and eddied up his nostrils. It was the goddamned tank! He was wedged in there because the space was too narrow for both his body and the tank! He gripped his knife with all the force of his body focused on his right hand, as the water sought to twist the knife from his grasp. Had to cut away the tank! The weight of the current against the cylinder pressed the straps against his shoulders. No way to slip the knife under. He must saw through the webbing directly against his chest.

White pain.

His pulse throbbed, expanding in his head. His throat convulsed for air. Cut harder! Cut, damn it!

The tank went, smashing his foot as it rushed out under him. He was moving again, twisting. The knife was gone. With a terrible crunching sound, something hit the back of his head. His diaphragm heaved within him, sucking for breath. His heartbeat hammered in his head as he tumbled and twisted in the chaos of foam and bubbles.

Bubbles . . . Foam! He could see! Swim up! Swim!

And that's how the chapter ends, leaving the reader almost as breathless as Trevanian's protagonist. Trevanian used a Series of Shots to get the best and most appropriate reaction from readers.

Use Series of Shots to Amplify Tension

Here's a great scene you might recall from the movie *The Fugitive* (screenplay by Jeb Stuart and David Twohy, 1993). This is the tense scene in which the bus carrying the dangerous convicts on the way to prison crashes onto the railroad tracks—and of course a train is coming and the hero, Kimble, has to get out.

This nail-biting scene is bursting with tension, but the screenwriters ramp it up by inserting a series of shots that shoot the tension into the stratosphere.

INT. BUS - NIGHT

Kimble spots keys. Pitches them to Old Guard. Drags Young Guard to the front for a quick exit. But Old Guard fumbles the key ring, his hands shaking as much as the bus.

The train light spiderwebs across cracked windows. Kimble snatches the keys away from the Guard's trembling hands.

> KIMBLE
> Which one? This? This one?!

Old Guard gulps a nod. Kimble jams a key in the lock. Throws the door open. Grabs Young Guard.

> KIMBLE
> Help me get him—

But Old Guard climbs right over Kimble's back and climbs out the shattered windshield.

ANGLE ON REAR OF BUS

Copeland escapes through the hole in the back...

EXT. BUS - NIGHT

... and hits the ground running the other way. The locomotive's headlight reveals the toppled bus.

INT. BUS - NIGHT

Train light grows. A nanosecond of uncertainty: Should Kimble leave the wounded man? Kimble and the Young Guard hold a look.

EXT. FREIGHT TRAIN - NIGHT

As the WHEELS BRAKE and LOCK.

EXT. RAILROAD TRACKS - NIGHT

Kimble struggles out of the bus - pulling the Young Guard behind him. He slings the man clear.

SCREECHING death, the TRAIN SKIDS closer.

For one heartbeat, Kimble remains perched atop the bus.

The train light X-rays him.

Kimble leaps. Lands. Rolls. Gains his feet. Tries to sprint away but can't: His feet are still chained. He gets off a dozen mincing steps before...

IMPACT: A hundred tons of STEEL SLAMS into the bus, splitting it open.

Shrapnel rips through Kimble's thigh, but he stays on his feet, still running feverish half-steps.

An EXPLOSION envelops the train. Flames stream down its flanks.

The train burns past the wounded Guard.

Kimble looks back, expecting to see the catastrophe behind him. But he gets the shock of his life - of any man's life:

Still on its wheels, the locomotive is derailing - and coming after him. It's the stuff of nightmares: One little man being chased by a fire-breathing locomotive.

The train burrows to a stop.

Kimble is suddenly five feet taller, standing
on an upheaval of earth, staring eyeball-to-
eyeball with the train that nearly devoured
him. He pants. Coughs on smoke. Then notices
something in his hand.

It's the key ring.

This Series of Shots comprises Close-Ups, Inserts, Medium Shots, and Long Shots, but these are all stationary camera shots. Instead of having the camera move and Follow or Pan Kimble as he works his way out of the bus and gets clear of the impending collision, this fast clip of visuals encompassing all the important elements of the scene packs the best punch to leave viewers breathless and gripping the arms of their chairs.

Alternating Scenes with a Series of Shots

Author Colum McCann, in his award-winning novel *Let the Great World Spin*, does a brilliant job by showing two scenes occurring at the same time—something tricky to do in a novel but easy in a film. The effect is wonderfully cinematic as the reader reads through this series of shots that alternates between two events happening at once in two different locales. McCann wanted to have the reader see both scenarios unfolding at the same time, rather than show one whole, complete scene with one set of characters, followed by another scene showing the others. It's a powerful effect that he's borrowed from film technique, and it supercharges his novel.

The narrator of this scene is Corrigan's brother. He's reflecting back on the accident Corrigan was in, thinking about where he himself was at the time. Without even breaking up the paragraph, McCann gives us this battery of shots:

They were sure he [Corrigan] was dead at first, and he was loaded in a meat wagon with Jazzlyn. A cough of blood alerted a paramedic. He was taken to a hospital on the East Side.

Who knows where we were, driving back, in another part of

the city, on a ramp, in a traffic jam, at a toll booth—does it matter? There was a little bubble of blood at my brother's mouth. We drove on, singing quietly, while the kids in the back seats dozed. Albee had solved a problem for himself. He called it a mutual checkmate. My brother was scooped into an ambulance, There was nothing we could have done to save him. No words that would have brought him back. It had been a summer of sirens. His was another. The lights spun. They took him to Metropolitan Hospital, the emergency room. Sprinted him down through the pale-green corridors. Blood on the floor behind them. Two thin tracks from the back trolled wheels. Mayhem all around. I dropped Adelita and her children outside the tiny clapboard house where they lived. She turned and looked over her shoulder at me, waved. She smiled. She was his. She would suit him. She was all right. He would find his God with her. My brother was wheeled into the triage room. Shouts and whispers. An oxygen mask over his face. Chest ripped open. A collapsed lunch. One-inch tubes inserted to keep him breathing. A nurse with a manual blood-pressure cuff. I sat at the wheel of the van and watched as the lights went on in Adelita's house. I saw her shape against the light curtains until heavier ones were drawn across. I started the engine. They held him in traction with counterweights above the bed. A single breathing machine by his bed. The flood so skiddy with blood that the interns had to wipe their feet.

All that in one paragraph. Although, this alternating series of shots continues for many more paragraphs, bringing both scenes to a head, as Corrigan's brother learns the grim news, then picks up Adelita and takes her to the hospital, where she rushes to Corrigan's bedside and sees him die.

So think about scenes you can construct in your novel that may benefit from a Series of Shots. Whether it's a fast-action scene in which a lot is happening and many details need to be shown or you want to speed up time and move quickly through the scene to get to your high moment, consider utilizing this powerful cinematic technique in your novel.

Chapter 7

The Punch Is in the Details

Insert, Angle On, Match Cut

Some of the stationary shots are brief but used purposefully. When reading screenplays, you may not see the directives Insert or Angle On, but the way the script is written implies this type of shot.

Take a look at the previous excerpt from *The Fugitive*. See where it reads "IMPACT: A hundred tons of STEEL SLAMS into the bus" and "It's the key ring"? These are Inserts.

With Insert, the idea is to *briefly* interrupt the action to home in on one specific thing that needs to be given full attention. It may not be visible in the current shot, as shown in this excerpt.

Inserts are mainly used in reference to objects like a clock, or actions, like putting a key in a car's ignition. The action before the impact of the train follows Kimble as he's limping away from the bus, so in order to cut to the crash behind him, the screenwriter uses an Insert to show this happening.

You'll see this in action/suspense movies and books. You're watching a car chase, and then you see a few seconds of the front wheel before cutting back to the car crashing. In a novel you might write: "The last bolt came loose and fell onto the road."

In other instances, an Insert shot can be the character abruptly noticing something that shifts the reader's attention. Perhaps he hears glass breaking and turns. The Insert shot would be the description of the plate-glass window shattering and glass flying into the room.

Remember Who's Witnessing the Action

It's important to remember to stay in your point-of-view character's head when inserting details this way. Movies, for the most part, give an outside POV, unless the screenwriter specifies the camera shot called POV, which means for the camera to behave as though it is seeing through the character's eyes (we'll go over that in more depth later). In a film, a director has license to jump from place to place to capture the action in the most effective way, and in sense the camera is the "outside observer." But unless you are writing a novel in an omniscient POV, which is not often done and is not easy to do well, you are limited to showing only what your character sees.

So if your POV character is in a car with the wheel about to fall off, she can only sense it by the movement of the car and the sounds she hears, or she has to look out her window and see the wheel wobbling.

Here's a good reason to think through who your POV character will be in a scene for the best effect. Sometimes it's an observer watching from a Full Shot or some other angle, who can best witness the events needed to be shown in your novel and whose reaction will heighten the tension and help advance the plot. Of course, if you are writing in first person, you are limited to only what your one character experiences, but you can find creative ways to show what needs to be shown in each scene through the use of various camera shots.

In that scene I excerpted from *Shibumi* in the previous chapter, Trevanian throws in a couple of well-placed Inserts. Remember that cracked faceplate on his diving mask? When Hel realizes his jaw his broken, he thinks "uh-oh" and that shifts his attention to his mask.

> He tugged it from its pouch and examined it in the light of his lamp, which was yellowing because the batteries were fading. The faceplate was cracked.
>
> It was a hairline crack. It might hold, so long as there was no wrench or torque on the rubber fittings. And what was the chance of that, down in the ripping current at the bottom of the Wine Cellar? Not much.

Many writers intuitively use Insert shots without much thought. If we're describing something happening in a scene, we will call attention to a detail that's important. But think about how you might do that, and instead of just *telling* that your character notices something, *show it* by inserting it in a way the reader can see it clearly.

It seems to imply a Close-Up, but an Insert could be a shot of the burning hot sun above beating down on a thirsty traveler in a desert. Or a bomber plane streaking through the sky aflame. If you were going to show a longer bit of action, like the plane continuing on over the landscape, burning and smoking, and the pilots ejecting, the script would use a Cut To and consider that another segment of filming rather than an Insert. Think "brief glimpse."

Angle On

This shot usually occurs in scenes taking place in large settings, and the purpose is to tell the director that the camera should be focused on one particular element in the group. For example: if your character is at a playground and is looking for her young daughter among a group of kids playing, to get from the Medium Shot, Long Shot, or Pan (as she's scanning the playground), you'd use "ANGLE ON STRUCTURE" to suggest a new shot featuring her daughter. The camera is still shooting stationary from the same location, but the director knows to point the camera in a different direction to lock on to what's important to be noticed. Again, it's all about telling the viewer to pay attention to what the writer wants noticed.

And novelists need to do the same. Let's say you're writing a scene in which your undercover detective is at a large party and has to keep a tail on someone. Your hero is standing by the punchbowl and watching his suspect talking across the room. You'll want to put in some description of the room and the guests attending—what they're doing, how they're dressed—but the focus is angled on the suspect and paying attention to what he's doing.

If you turn back a few pages to the excerpt from *The Fugitive*, you'll see the directive to "angle on the rear of the bus" as Copeland gets away. The camera has shifted from Kimble to show this important bit—that Copeland has escaped. It's like an Insert, but instead of a brief shot of an object or instant, with Angle On, the camera is rolling and we're watching from this new angle.

So think about places in your novel when you have scenes of crowds, or where a lot is going on around your character. This is where you can use this camera shot to have your character watch something

73

specific, which will make it stand out and clue the reader by saying "Pay attention: something important is happening here."

Who can forget the powerful moment at the end of *American Beauty*? The teenage girlfriend of Lester's daughter has come into the kitchen and talks briefly with him before leaving, and the viewer just knows what's about to happen. Notice how important this Angle On is at the climax of the story.

ANGELA
How are you?

LESTER
(smiles,taken aback)

God, it's been a long time since anybody asked
me that.

(thinks about it)

I'm great.

They just sit there, smiling at each other, then:

ANGELA
(suddenly)
I've gotta go to the bathroom.

She crosses off. Lester watches her go, then stands there wondering why he should suddenly feel so content.

LESTER
(laughs)

I'm great.

Something at the edge of the counter catches his eye, and he reaches for...

CLOSE on a framed PHOTOGRAPH as he picks it up: It's the photo we saw earlier of him, Carolyn, and Jane, taken several years ago at an amusement park. It's startling how happy they look.

Lester crosses to the kitchen table, where he sits and studies the photo. He suddenly seems older, more mature... and then he smiles: the deep, satisfied smile of a man who just now understands the punch line of a joke he heard long ago...

                    LESTER (CONT'D)

              Man oh man...

                  (softly)

              Man oh man oh man...

After a beat, the barrel of a GUN rises up behind his head, aimed at the base of his skull.

ANGLE ON an arrangement of fresh-cut ROSES in a vase on the opposite counter, deep crimson against the WHITE TILE WALL. Then a GUNSHOT suddenly rings out, ECHOING unnaturally. Instantly, the tile is sprayed with BLOOD, the same deep crimson as the roses.

Don't underestimate the power of a single lasting image at the end of a scene. Using Angle On may be just the shot (pun intended) you need to supercharge that moment.

Match Cuts for Creative Structure

I'm including a shot called a Match Cut in here although it's not often used. A Match Cut is a cut in film editing between either two different objects, two different spaces, or two different compositions in which an object in the two shots graphically match, often helping to establish a strong continuity of action and linking the two shots metaphorically.

The most famous example used to describe a Match Cut is the scene in the beginning of the movie *2001: A Space Odyssey*, in which an ape throws a bone into the air after discovering its potential as a weapon, which then turns end over end. The Match Cut replaces the bone with a much more advanced weapon: an orbiting nuclear weapons satellite.

A Match Cut occurs at the end of Alfred Hitchcock's *North by Northwest*. As Cary Grant pulls Eva Marie Saint up from Mount Rushmore, the cut then goes to him pulling her up to his bunk on the train. The Match Cut here jumps past the courting, the marriage proposal, and the actual marriage of the two characters who, for much of the film, had been adversaries.

Let's say you have a scene in which a man is in a jewelry store picking out an engagement ring. You could have the scene end with him holding up the ring and declaring this is the one. Then, with a scene break, you could create a Match Cut effect by opening with his fiancée holding the same ring up, pulling back to show her with her best friend as she gushes over the ring.

In Bryan Litfin's fantasy novel *The Gift*, he uses a Match Cut in a creative way. The scene opens with Ana at a creek with two others. A snake suddenly wraps around her ankle and yanks her into the water, and for some reason, the couple she is with abandons her as she cries for help.

> The water was up to Ana's chin now. She tried to keep herself afloat, but it was no use. The tightness around her chest stifled her breath. Ana threw her head back to keep her mouth above the water.
>
> "No! Please! I want to go with you! Help me!"
>
> The man and woman disappeared into the forest. Murky water closed over Ana's head.
>
> She shrieked with all her strength.
>
> It was dark. Every sense was alive, yet Ana understood nothing. She panted with quick, shallow breaths. Her heart raced. She clutched cloths in her hands.
>
> *Where am I?*

Slowly awareness of her surroundings returned. She was sitting up in bed. The sheets were twisted around her ankles.

The door burst open "Anastasia! Are you okay?" It was Vanita.

"I'm—I'm—" Ana wasn't she what she was.

"Oh, honey, you had a terrible nightmare!"

Litfin uses this creative technique nicely, shifting Ana out of her nightmare and into wakefulness with the Match Cut—first showing the snake wrapped around her ankles, then cutting to the sheets wrapped around her. Much nicer than just saying, "Ana jerked awake. Oh, she was only having a nightmare!"

Use Match Cuts with Symbols and Motifs

Think about the metaphors or motifs you may be using in your novel. A powerful way to drive home the symbolism of a metaphor is to use a Match Cut. If a dark forest and scary trees symbolize fear in a horror story, and the character always feels the trees are watching her, why not do a Match Cut from a dark tree that startles your character to the real scary guy hiding behind her house, who is tall and in the dark could be mistaken for a tree? It might go something like this:

Trudy pulled her coat up tight against her neck, the imposing trees lining the abandoned lane towering over her, their spindly arms extended as if reaching to grab her.

She broke into a run, barely able to see in the dim light of the sliver of moonlight. Her breath stuck in her throat; she tripped over roots pushing up through the cracks in the old asphalt, then righted herself and pushed on, the trees watching, listening, waiting . . .

He stood behind the shed in the dark, watching, listening, waiting—just another shadow among the trees. He heard her coming and stretched out his arms, ready to grab her. *Any moment now . . .*

Even though this isn't an exact Match Cut, you get the idea. In a novel you can play up motifs and metaphors in ways films sometimes can't. This is where the beauty of words can oftentimes evoke more than a visual image can.

Later, we'll be looking at how to use camera shots in a figurative, conceptual sense rather than a strictly visual one. And what I hope you will come to realize as we look deeper into these cinematic secrets is that words can sometimes show *more* than a film can, in many ways.

And now, Cut To: Moving Shots.

Part 2

Moving Shots

SIGNS

Screenplay by M. Night Shyamalan, 2002

> BOY (O.S.)
> Dad!

Graham looks in the direction of THE BOY'S VOICE. He's close. Graham picks up Bo and rushes through the crops.

He finds MORGAN standing with his hands in the pockets of his pajama bottoms. DOGS ARE BARKING NEARBY.

> GRAHAM
> Morgan what's happening?

Graham puts Bo on the ground and moves right in front of Morgan. The ten-year old boy looks deep in thought.

Graham takes hold of Morgan's chin and turns his face so he's looking straight at him.

>   GRAHAM
>   Are...you...hurt?

Beat. Morgan's eyes reveal he's come to some answer.

>   MORGAN
>   I think God did it.

Beat. THE DOGS KEEP BARKING.

>   GRAHAM
>   Did what Morgan?

Morgan takes hold of his father's unshaven chin and turns his face. Graham is forced to look to his right. Beat. Graham sees something.

Graham Hess slowly rises to his feet. He starts moving forward towards something.

He walks through a thin layer of crops and emerges in a clearing. Two German Shepherds are running back and forth. They are clearly agitated.

Graham looks around at the THOUSANDS OF CORN STALKS LYING FLAT ON THE GROUND. THEY LAY IN A GIGANTIC CIRCLE, A HUNDRED FEET WIDE.

Graham Hess looks around in a daze as he walks out into the center. Merrill, Bo, and Morgan follow him.

The dogs keep running and barking as WE PULL BACK AND REVEAL THE FOUR MEMBERS OF THE HESS FAMILY STANDING IN THE MIDDLE OF THIS PERFECT GIGANTIC CIRCLE.

WE KEEP PULLING BACK TO EXPOSE THIS EERIE DESIGN—FIVE HUNDRED FEET WIDE—SITTING IN THE MIDDLE OF AN ENDLESS UNTOUCHED CORNFIELD.

Camera shots in motion are dynamic and fluid. They can follow the action with the velocity of a train or move as slow as a turtle, pulling back to reveal something shocking. Moving shots mimic the way our eyes follow what's happening, and are the most powerful way writers can lead a reader to notice the things she wants noticed. The right choice of a moving shot will effect pacing and tension, and with the right moving shots, the high moment of a scene will be supercharged with power.

It's important to keep in mind the distinction between a movie and a novel when it comes to the moving camera. In a novel, the POV character is the camera, and so the way the scene is "shot" through the character's eyes mimics the various camera shots.

It's more about the attention and focus rather than the literal movement. A character doesn't need to walk closer to something to zoom in. Neither does he have to run along a road to be panning the action being observed as he's watching the killer get away. These "camera shots" can be happening all in his head while he is physically stationary.

In addition, we'll explore the more figurative use of moving shots—functioning more as metaphor. Novelists have a wonderful medium in which to translate moving shots into powerful prose.

Chapter 8

Homing In on a Key Moment

Zoom, Zoom, Zoom

Zooming in to look at something close up is a natural behavior. We do it all the time, every day. For those of us who regularly misplace our glasses, we may zoom in especially close to an object to see it clearly. We zoom into maps on the Internet to get a better idea of where we are going. So, too, with the Zoom shot in screenplays. There is no better way to tell a viewer to watch closely than to zoom in. The purpose of a Zoom Shot is to progressively change the emphasis of the focus on something previously unseen or unnoticed so that it now becomes the key element of the segment, to the exclusion of other, outside competing elements.

Many writers set up their "camera" in one spot and never move it. Even with their camera stuck in place, they may have a powerful scene. But how much more charged would some of these static scenes be if the writer deliberately used a Zoom shot to call attention to something important? If we want to take our scenes from ordinary to extraordinary, we need to supercharge them by utilizing dynamic technique, and using a Zoom is one great way to do so.

Larger Than Life

In screenwriting, the camera shot Zoom really means to make something larger than life-size, and students of cinematography are told not to mistake a Zoom with a Push In, indicating the camera is to move closer to an object. These days you rarely see the word *Zoom* in a script to indicate that as a camera shot. But there are also many ways cameramen (and women) can get closer to the action, using such things as dolly shots (a camera mounted on a moving dolly), tracking shots, and handheld cameras like the Steadicam. However, for fiction writing purposes, I'm not going to differentiate or get too specific, for if a character in a novel draws close to an object or person to see it close up, how can the reader know that the POV character is seeing something larger than life or that a dolly shot is being used instead of a Steadicam?

Sure, by the minute detail she notices, like a speck on a contact lens, the reader might get that sense, but for all intents and purposes, it's not important to differentiate. So we'll just use Zoom for the overall moving of a camera in close to its target. You can make the distinction in your scene just how close by what kinds of details your character notices.

Zooming In Builds Tension

Zoom shots are powerful. I personally love using Zoom and Pull Back (the opposite, which we'll cover next) more than any other shots. Why? Because they are so dynamic. How better to pinpoint exactly what you want the reader to notice than by zooming in? Although a Close Shot can do the same, the fact that the camera is *moving* toward the object you want the reader to notice builds tension.

Think about it. You can either cut to the dead body lying on the kitchen floor, or you can start with your character at the threshold of the door, with a Long Shot, seeing something that looks like blood on the tile. Then as she inches closer, the camera Pans (i.e., your character nervously looking around to see if anyone is there), and then zooms in on the body, getting closer and closer, seeing more and more detail, until your character sees who it is and screams. Or something like that.

Homing In on the Details

In the movie *The Bourne Identity*, screenwriter Tony Gilroy gives us a Series of Shots that gradually zoom in closer and closer until the important items for the scene are shown. Although this feels predominately like a Close-Up, we draw in close as Castel moves from the door to the pile of books, then the camera homes in on the box and then what's inside the box. The high moment for this segment of scene is the revealing of the contents of the box.

INT. STORAGE WAREHOUSE ELEVATOR -- DAY

CASTEL and THE ELEVATOR OPERATOR -- rising slowly through the dark warehouse and --

INT. CASTEL'S STORAGE UNIT -- DAY

Darkness -- a key turning -- door opening -- light goes on to reveal CASTEL standing there and we're in --

CASTEL'S STORAGE UNIT. What's in here? Like nothing. Like a stack of old newspapers in the corner. Some mildewed books piled along one wall. Some shitty plastic chairs.

QUICK TIME CUTS

CASTEL working fast. Closing the door. Moving to the pile of books. Taking the top book off. Opening it.

INSIDE THE BOX -- a timer. A small bomb. A booby-trap. An LED light stops flashing as CASTEL'S HANDS code in his password and --

CASTEL moving to the newspapers stacked in the corner. Pulling away the top pile and --

A METAL LOCK BOX. Hidden here. CASTEL pulling it out. Opening it. An empty tray on top and --

CASTEL taking off his watch. Taking off his rings. Taking out his wallet. His Spanish passport. Emptying his pockets. All of this goes into the empty tray and --

CASTEL lifting away this top tray -- setting it aside and --

THE METAL LOCK BOX -- there's more -- a much larger bottom compartment -- and it's déjà-vu all over again -- we're looking at the identical contents we saw Bourne find in the Zurich safe-deposit box.

First of all...

MONEY. Lots of it. Ten thousand dollar stacks of hundreds. Lots of them. A GUN. A very good gun. A dozen clips of ammo. And FIVE MORE PASSPORTS. All clean. Brand-new. All with his photo. Five different names. Four different countries. Each one of these pristine clipped to a piece of card stock that says:

NAME:
NATIONALITY:
PLACE OF ISSUE:
SIGNATURE SAMPLE:
A BAR CODE:

Two Italian. Two Spanish. A Portuguese.

CASTEL going for the Portuguese passport and - CUT TO:

EXT. ALPS HELICOPTER SHOT -- DAY

The little red car driving through The Alps.

Think, then, about scenes in your novel in which an important detail needs to be shown or revealed. Instead of just showing it or talking about it, think how you can start your "camera" further back, giving a more general overview of what is happening with your character, then narrowing both your character's attention and the camera's focus to move in closer and pay attention to something "small" that needs to be magnified.

This is the power of the Zoom shot, and it will supercharge your scenes.

Pairing Literal with Figurative

In Meg Moseley's debut novel *When Sparrows Fall*, we watch her two main characters holding a discussion in a barn. The scene starts off with a Full Shot of the two of them. A lot of writers would leave the camera there and "shoot" the entire scene from that one angle. But Moseley doesn't. She very deliberately, at just the right moment, zooms in on what's crucial to the scene—the revelation Jack will come to—which is a vital element of the novel. By pushing that camera in close to see the small details, the scene is powerful. In fact, almost every time I read this segment in my workshop, I get choked up—because I know the import of the moment. But it's also because Moseley does a terrific job building to her high moment.

> Jack moved to the doorway. Leaning against the massive timbers, he studied her profile. Her lower lip trembled.
>
> "What about the children?" he asked, assailed by vague fears. "Why do you mention them and Mason in the same breath?"
>
> She faced into the gloom of the barn again, silhouetted against the sunset. "It's nothing sordid."
>
> "What is it?" He moved closer, wishing physical proximity could help him drag the truth out of her. "Tell me."
>
> Breathing fast and shallow, she said nothing.
>
> He realized he was framing her, as if he were the photographer now. Memorizing her. In case she sent him away for being a bully. In case he never saw her again.
>
> The sun caught the quilt on her shoulder in a golden spotlight. The fabrics in the wide border of the quilt didn't quite match the worn and faded fabrics in the center section. In one corner of the center piece, the sun highlighted small holes where someone had pulled out stitches that must have been made with thick thread. The stitches had left ghosts of themselves, perhaps the remnants of lettering. Like the names she'd embroidered on crib quilts.
>
> Drawn closer still, Jack traced the ghost-stitches with one finger. Seven or eight letters, maybe.
>
> He stopped breathing.

Everywhere, sets of seven. Seven dried roses in the wreath on the door. Sets of seven drawn on the cover of the attendance book. Six angels in the Christmas cupboard and one more hidden in the kitchen. Six baby quilts, and this one—but only six children.

"Dear God," he said.

Miranda said nothing.

Now here's something to consider. Jack draws close; the camera pushes in. What he sees in this Extreme Close-Up startles him with realization. And what that triggers, essentially, is a *mental* Pull Back. He doesn't literally back away, but his awareness pulls back to encompass a bigger picture. As he pieces together the bits of information that lead him to his startling conclusion, the bigger, overarching plot elements of the novel come into focus.

There are few moments more profound in novels than the ones in which a character starts seeing the "big picture." When a novelist utilizes a figurative Pull Back expertly, he's created a powerful, unforgettable moment. And we'll look at this in more detail in the next chapter.

Chapter 9

Open the Reader's Eyes and Heart

Pull Back for Revelation

Take a look at this trademark scene in *Jurassic Park* (one of my favorites!) that you surely recall if you saw the movie. Notice how the camera shots change from close to closer until at Extreme Close-Up, but then, Crichton punches home by using a Pull Back to show full damage for greatest impact.

EXT NEDRY'S JEEP, BACK ROADS -

Nedry speeds along the rain-slick road, fishtailing as he goes.

CLOSE ON - Nedry at the wheel.

NEDRY'S POV - the dark, wet road running alongside a ten-foot chain-link fence. Suddenly, a beast-like visage blurs across the road.

Nedry swerves. The jeep skids. Nedry tries to over-steer, can't bring the careening jeep under control.

The jeep crashes though the fence, bounces down a cement culvert, and dives into a raging gully.

Nedry curses. He spins the wheel. The tires spin and spray. The jeep's hopelessly stuck in the gully. From Nedry's seat in the jeep, he cranes his head around, examining his situation.

NEDRY'S POV - On the opposite side of the gully, there is an equipment graveyard. By the titled jeep headlights, steely monsters all around can be seen - discarded earth movers, graders, and tractors.

Nedry gets out of the jeep, grabs the winch from the jeep's back end, and wades over to an abandoned tractor.

                    NEDRY
Shit. I'm going to have to change clothes.

He loops the winch around the tractor's base. Suddenly, he stops and looks around as he hears a gentle HOOTING. He squints, looking at the strange steel graveyard lit by the bright beams of the jeep headlights.

HOOT! HOOT! A distinctive HOOTING. Nedry looks up in fear. SILENCE.

Nedry starts moving toward his jeep. Again, the HOOT! Nedry stops, looks right, looks left. A RUSTLE in the trees. Nedry's head cocks.

Looking through trees, lit by the strong beams, Nedry sees a SPITTER in the eerie mist. Now it's gone. Now it's back. It circles Nedry warily, hunting him. Nedry stares.

NEDRY
I hope this is one of them herbivores.

Nedry scrambles the other way, full-tilt. Hop, hop, and the Spitter drops in front of Nedry from the other side. HOOT!

Nedry jumps back, lands on his butt. The Spitter zips in from the side - HOOT!

Nedry doubles back, racing through the abandoned equipment, ducking and rolling under a cement mixer, spinning past a tree. He splashes down the embankment, trying to get to his jeep. He uses the winch line to steady himself again the raging current. He finally reaches the jeep, swings open the door - and, surging out of the water like a demonic apparition, is the SPITTER! Nedry backs away, directly into the glare of the headlights!

CLOSE ON - the Spitter. Its plume opens; bright orange gills swell out like an umbrella around its neck. Something squirts beneath its jaws.

A big glob SMACKS Nedry on the arm. He brushes it off.

NEDRY
Gross.

EXTREME CLOSE-UP - the Spitter's head. The jaws puff, the hood flares out, the neck snaps forward. And - it spits.

This glob misses Nedry, splashes off the steaming headlight.

VERY EXTREME CLOSE-UP - The Spitter's swollen poison sacs are inflated. They fire!

This glob hits Nedry in the eyes. He SCREAMS.

                    NEDRY
            I'm blind, I'm blind.

He falls against the jeep, rubbing his eyes. The Spitter calmly hops to the embankment and watches the blinded Nedry weave drunkenly in the water. Nedry grabs on to the jeep and pulls himself along toward the driver's door. The Spitter stalks, watching him.

Nedry pulls open the jeep door, thrusts his head in, slams it against the door frame. Now Nedry heaves his whole body into the jeep. The Spitter's long ostrich-like legs stretch and bend in an easy gait as it closes it on Nedry.

Nedry sits behind the wheel, unseeing as the Spitter watches patiently, turns his blind eyes that way.

A long beat. The Spitter leaps forward, the CAMERA PULLS BACK WIDER AND WIDER. Nedry lets out an ear-splitting SCREAM and the car horn BLARES.

Crichton doesn't name camera shots for all the action going on, but we can picture the camera at a Full Shot watching as Nedry gets attacked. And in that final wider shot, we see the scene laid out before us: Nedry in the car screaming, the Spitter outside the car with something like a victorious look on its face, the jeep in the mud in the gulley, stuck and at an angle, its headlights glaring into the gloom. We shake our heads and feel sorry for the guy. Or maybe not.

Pulling Back Gives a Sense of Finality

Here's another brief example from *The Constant Gardener*—a scene beginning with a Close-Up, then pulling back briefly to make an emotional statement.

Pull Backs are all about revelation and emotional punch. This scene shows Sandy Woodrow, a man who works with the protagonist Justin Quayle and who had secretly been hopelessly in love with Justin's wife. After Tessa's death, Woodrow is desperate to find a letter he had sent her, fearful that Justin might stumble upon it. We see him here rummaging through Justin's office drawers.

> Old Christmas cards. Old invitations cards marked with a cross for "no" in Tessa's hand. Others, more emphatically marked "never." Old get-well card from Ghita Pearson, portraying Indian birds. A twist of ribbon, a wine cork, a bunch of diplomats' calling cards held together with a bulldog clip. But no small single sheet of HM stationery Office blue, ending with the triumphant scrawl: "I love you, and I love you, and I love you, Sandy."
>
> Woodrow sidled swiftly along the last shelves, flipping open books at random, opening trinket boxes, acknowledging defeat.

In this short narrative we get the sense of all the insignificant things Woodrow encounters in his frantic search. Instead of just saying he gave up in frustration, Le Carré uses a Pull Back from the intimacy of the desk to show Woodrow moving along the shelves, and with those last two words leaves us knowing just how his character feels.

A Big Aha Moment

Remember, Pull Backs are all about revelation and emotional reveal. Novelists wanting to use a metaphoric exclamation mark in a scene will do well to consider using this camera shot.

Yes, Close-Ups can reveal important details and provide *aha* moments. But Pull Backs are where the realization and understanding are shown. This is the place the writer pulls plot elements together, giving a wider scope of understanding of the overall story being told. Your character can zoom in to a clue and see it close up, while doing a mental Pull Back upon realizing this clue has just helped her solve the crime.

Picture a scene in which a character is staring at her hands as she kneels next to a body she's just found in her kitchen. She sees blood on her fingers. Then, the camera (her attention, purview) pulls back to show blood on the floor all around her, triggering a reaction to this "bigger" discovery. It may then pull back even further to include the entire room, which carries her scream throughout the house.

M. Night Shyamalan is a master at shocking and surprising moments created by the use of just the right camera shot, and he often uses a Pull Back for dramatic effect.

Remember the bit of one of the opening scenes in the movie SIGNS by Shyamalan (2002) that we saw earlier? Rather than beginning with an Establishing Shot showing just where his characters are, Shyamalan wants to surprise the viewer with a supercharged moment. I imagine him thinking about his high moment—the moment of revelation in which we see the "big picture" of what is really happening in this scene—and determining he wants to pull back to gradually reveal this. In order to build to this moment, he chooses more close-up shots to lead in, keeping the viewer in tension wondering what is going on and only seeing a bit of the setting. Shyamalan does a great job using cinematic technique to create suspense and then paying off the high moment with a pull back—showing the huge crop circle.

This scene is key to setting up the premise of the movie—the invasion of aliens on Earth. Although this movie is really not about aliens at all. The title —*Signs*—is a motif, and the "signs" of alien activity in Graham's cornfield, as well as all over the world, serve as signs of something much larger, and much more important. The Pull Back here in the beginning of the movie puts emphasis on the signs uncovered and sets the stage for the movie's plot, theme, and motifs. A truly important "aha" moment that uses the powerful camera shot Pull Back.

In another telling high moment, in the movie *The Sixth Sense* (1999), we watch Cole, the boy with this "sixth sense" explain (and prove) to his mother he can see and communicate with the dead. When their car is stopped due to an accident up ahead, Cole takes this moment to be brave and reveal to his mother his "gift." The Pull Back at the end of the conversation packs a powerful punch, like an exclamation mark to his confession.

```
                        COLE
          You know that accident up there?
```

>   LYNN
>   (confused)
>
>   Yeah.

>   COLE
>   Someone got hurt.

>   LYNN
>   They did?

>   COLE
>   A lady. She died.

>   LYNN
>   Oh my God.

Lynn leans over the steering wheel. She wipes the windshield with her palm to see better.

>   LYNN
>   You can see her?

>   COLE
>   Yes.

Lynn gazes out the windshield at the line of red taillights. Beat.

>   LYNN
>   Where is she?

>   COLE
>   Standing next to my window.

A WOMAN IN HER LATE FORTIES, HELMET CRACKED, HAIR MATTED WITH RAIN AND BLOOD, STANDS STARING THROUGH COLE'S PASSENGER WINDOW.

Lynn looks over slowly. She doesn't see anything outside his window. She eyes Cole.

> LYNN
> Cole, you're scaring me.

> COLE
> They scare me too sometimes.

> LYNN
> They?

> COLE
> Dead people.

> LYNN
> Dead people?

> COLE
> Ghosts.

Beat.

> LYNN
> You see ghosts, Cole?

> COLE
> They want me to do things for them.

> LYNN
> They talk to you?

Cole nods "Yes."

> LYNN
> They tell you to do things?

Cole nods "Yes" again. Lynn becomes upset. She nods with grave understanding. Cole watches her.

> COLE
> What are you thinking, Momma?

> LYNN
> ...I don't know.

                    COLE
            You think I'm a freak?

Lynn's eyes moves to Cole.

                    LYNN
             Look at my face.

Cole gazes at her intense expression.

                    LYNN
        I would never think that about you
             ... ever... Got it?

                    COLE
               Got it.

BEAT. Cole smiles a tiny smile. Lynn glances
down.

                    LYNN
        Just let me think for a second.

She drowns in her thoughts. Beat.

                    COLE
            Grandma says hi.

Lynn looks up sharply.

                    COLE
        She says she's sorry for taking the
        bumble bee pendant. She just likes
        it a lot.

                    LYNN
                What?

                    COLE
        Grandma comes to visit me sometimes.

Lynn becomes still. Her face is unreadable.
When she speaks, her words are extremely
controlled.

> LYNN
>> Cole, that's very wrong. Grandma's
>> gone. You know that.

> COLE
>> I know.

Beat.

> COLE
>> She wanted me to tell you—

> LYNN
>> (soft)
>> Cole, please stop.

> COLE
>> She wanted me to tell you, she saw
>> you dance.

Lynn's eyes lock on Cole's.

> COLE
>> She said when you were little, you
>> and her had a fight right before
>> your dance recital. You thought
>> she didn't come to see you dance.
>> She did.

Lynn brings her hands to her mouth.

> COLE
>> She hid in the back so you wouldn't
>> see... She said you were like an
>> angel.

Lynn begins to cry.

                    COLE
          She said, you came to her where
          they buried her. Asked her a
          question ... She said the answer is
          "Every day."

Lynn covers her face with her hands. The tears
roll out through her fingers.

                    COLE
                 (whispers)
             What did you ask?

Beat. Lynn looks at her son. She barely gets
the words out.

                    LYNN
                  (crying)
             Do I make her proud?

Cole moves closer to Lynn. She cradles him in
her arms. Mother and son hold each other tight.

WE PULL BACK FROM THE WINDSHIELD, BACK PAST THE
FRONT BUMPER WHERE THE FIGURE OF THE BLOODED
WOMAN STANDS STARING AT COLE AND HIS MOTHER.

WE SEE A MANGLED BIKE PULLED OUT FROM THE REAR-
ENDED CAR ON THE SIDEWALK. WE MOVE UP AND AWAY
FROM THE RAIN-SOAKED BRIDGE.

By pulling away from this very important moment between
mother and son, a key plot moment in the movie, it gives the viewer
some space to process the far-reaching effect of Cole's revelation to
her. We Pull Back and see confirmed this "other world" that Cole truly
sees, with the dead woman staring at Cole as witness to their very live,
human moment, and then the camera pulls back even more to show
the "ordinary world" as it continues on clueless to the spirit world
interfacing invisibly with it. Life—or death, in this case—goes on.

The Big Reveal

I would be remiss if I didn't include the famous final camera shot in the classic movie *The Planet of the Apes* (1967, screenplay by Michael Wilson). I'm sure everyone who saw this movie, even if it's been decades, remembers the powerful reveal of the last few seconds of the movie, which sure shocked me as a kid. No other movie says it better: Use a Pull Back for revelation.

CLOSER ANGLE - TRACKING WITH TAYLOR AND NOVA.

As they round the promontory, the tip of a strange rock formation comes into view. It appears to be jutting from the sea.

REACTION SHOT - TAYLOR

He reins in momentarily, baffled by what he sees. Then he rides on.

THE STRANGE FORMATION - AS SEEN BY TAYLOR

An immense column juts from the beach at a thirty-degree angle. We can now see that it is not rock, but metal. Green metallic tints show through its gray salt-stained surface. As we draw closer, the object takes on the appearance of a massive arm, its top shaped like a hand holding a torch.

REVERSE ANGLE - FAVORING TAYLOR

Frowning with consternation. His horse proceeds at a slow walk.

TRACKING WITH TAYLOR - WHAT HE SEES:

Near the base of the column, where the shore and water meet, are a row of metal spikes. From this angle they look like tank traps.

CLOSER - TAYLOR

Dumbfounded, he slides from his saddle, approaches the spikes. Nova dismounts and follows him.

                    TAYLOR
              (a cry of agony)
                My God!

He falls to his knees, buries his head in his hands. CAMERA SLOWLY DRAWS BACK AND UP to a HIGH ANGLE SHOT disclosing what Taylor has found. Half-buried in the sand and washed by the waves is the Statue of Liberty.

                                    FADE OUT
              THE END

So, think of Pull Backs for your "aha" moments. They provide the moment of realization, of getting the bigger picture, of revealing something important. Whether for a literal reveal or an emotional one, Pull Backs are camera shots that pack a punch and if used wisely, will supercharge your novel.

Chapter 10

Take the Reader Where You Want Her to Go

Pan, Follow, Find

Writing a novel is challenging. It's tough work and tricky, and here's one reason. With a movie or TV show, what you see is what you get. The picture is painted for you—every detail. And there is only one camera shot used at a time—unless you have some neat split-screen action happening, which is rare.

You watch as a character moves through the scene, talking or in action, and unless you are hearing a voice over (V.O.), you don't know her thoughts or what she is noticing. With a POV camera shot, the camera will be at the level of her eyes and looking around to imitate what she might see. But you still don't know what she is thinking or feeling while this scene is playing out.

Now, think about a novel. Often writers are doing the same thing—showing the scene with the POV character talking, walking, experiencing life. From one angle or another, we "watch" her as the scene plays out. But in addition, a novel works simultaneously on a subsurface level. There's a camera inside the character's head at all times, and often it's necessary or desired to reveal what that camera is aimed at.

Wait, that's a bit confusing! It can be, and often trips up inexperienced writers. It's a juggling act of great finesse to execute a scene in which the reader is *watching the action* (which includes the POV character herself) as well as experiencing *being in the character's head*. Great writers constantly toggle back and forth from deep POV observations, whether visual or abstract (emotional, conceptual thoughts), and the larger scene action as a whole.

Readers Are Used to Being Schizophrenic

Readers are used to experiencing this rather schizophrenic structure. In fact, we are so used to it that it feels natural. Our own interaction with our world is reflected in this.

Think how in a matter of moments, inside our head, we jump from what we are doing right now to a memory of something that happened in the past, to thoughts about what we are going to do next year. All the while we are engaged in some activity—cooking dinner, holding a conversation with our spouse (okay, only women can do these two things at the same time, according to my husband), or driving around lost looking for a street sign.

Just how do we multitask like this? Who knows. But it is natural.

And so our scenes should imitate real life—but hopefully filtered to take out all the boring bits and chaotic nonsense.

It makes me think of that scene in *Being John Malkovich*, in which one of the characters is briefly inside Malkovich's mind and seeing out his eyes. It's a mundane scene that takes place in the kitchen, with Malkovich on the phone ordering some towels from a catalog while grabbing some leftover Chinese food from the fridge.

Of course, the guy who has the few moments inside Malkovich's head is ecstatic over the experience, but the irony and humor is in the fact that what he witnessed was about as boring and mundane as can be. Which is what a lot of our thoughts and actions are.

But we don't want those bits in our novel. We want every thought and action to be significant—not necessarily hugely important but contributing to the overall "painting" we are creating that tells the story we mean to tell.

So keep this in mind as you take a look at novels and the camera shots they are using.

Pay attention to how great writers balance the external and internal cameras to portray a "holistic" and rich scene for the reader.

This is especially evident in moving shots that follow the character along.

Pan to Take It All In

What's a Pan? No, not the things in your kitchen. A Pan is used by the screenwriter to tell the camera to move from one place to another. Pan stands for *panoramic* and implies the camera pivoting while mounted or on a tripod. A Pan operates in real time, showing how long it takes or how far a character has to move across a space, and it can show the spatial relationships that exist in the story.

Pan left, Pan right. Why? To get the reader to shift focus and draw her attention to some detail. It emphasizes the character noticing something. This can include Angle On, which focuses in on one aspect of a larger scene; for example, an Establishing Shot may show a large park with a playground. The camera might Pan across the park, then Angle On the merry-go-round, where we see a little girl crying. A writer could just start the scene saying "a little girl sat crying on a merry-go-round." But how much more visual power does it give to have your POV character enter the park, and then their "inner camera" does what the movie camera would do. The impact of the POV character's eyes alighting on this distressed child reveals more about her character as we watch her notice the girl and react.

In Kim Edwards's novel *the Memory Keeper's Daughter*, we watch her character, Caroline, look around her room after David leaves. This is a pivotal moment in her life, and she's aware how things now look different.

> He left then, and everything was the same as it had been: the clock on the mantel, the square of light on the floor, the sharp shadows of bare branches. In a few weeks the new leaves would come, feathering out on the trees and changing the shapes on the floors. She had seen all this so many times, and yet the room seemed strangely impersonal now, as if she had never lived here at all. . . . Leave all of it, she supposed, looking around at the framed prints of landscapes, the wicker magazine rack by the sofa, the low coffee table. Her own apartment seemed suddenly no more personal than a waiting room in any clinic in any town.

We don't just see the items in the room—we see the emotional response of her character seeing these things as the camera Pans. Edwards mimics the way we might notice things around us, with Caroline lingering on the thoughts of how the trees will change through the seasons, then her attention moving across the prints and furnishings, leaving her with a *feeling*. And this is what good writers do—use the camera to point out specific details—but for a purpose: to lead the reader to an emotional response, heightened and amplified by specific camera technique.

A terrific example of a beautifully cinematic Pan in a novel scene is this one in Charles Martin's novel *When Crickets Cry*. Martin's character is standing on a sidewalk watching a little girl who is selling lemonade at a makeshift stand. We don't know barely anything about his POV character telling this story, but through the narrative, much is revealed.

Martin is a master at microtension, cluing the reader in on the important pieces of the story one small bit at a time, raising questions as he answers them. Look at how and where he positions his camera, and then how it Pans, creating a tension that builds and builds as the reader begins to understand what terrible thing is about to happen. Instead of starting the action where the key moment occurs, he begins far away, with a breeze—and the camera tags along with that breeze, playing a key "character" role in what is to come.

A strong breeze fell down through the hills and blew east up Savannah Street. It ripped along the old brick buildings, up the sidewalk, through squeaky weather vanes and melodious wind chimes and across Annie's lemonade stand, where it picked up her Styrofoam cup and scattered almost ten dollars in change and currency across the street. She hopped off her folding chair and began chasing the paper money into the intersection.

I saw it too late, and she never saw it at all.

A bread delivery truck traveling right past me down South Main caught a green light and accelerated, creating a backfire and puff of white smoke. I could hear its radio playing bluegrass and see the driver stuffing a Twinkie into his mouth as he turned through the intersection and held up his hand to block the sun. Then he must have seen the yellow of Annie's dress. He slammed on the brakes, locked up the back tires, and began spinning and hopping sideways. The farther the truck turned sideways, the more the tires hopped atop the asphalt.

Annie turned to face the noise and froze. She dropped the money in her hand, which fluttered across the street like monarch butterflies, and lost control of her bladder. She never made a peep because the tightness in her throat squelched any sound.

The driver screamed, "Oh, sweet Jesus, Annie!" He turned the wheel as hard as it would turn and sent the back bumper of the truck into the right-front panel of a parked Honda Accord. The truck deflected off the Honda just before the flat side of the panel truck hit Annie square in the chest. The noise of her body hitting the hollow side of that truck sounded like a cannon.

She managed to raise one hand, taking most of the blow, and began rolling backward like a yellow bowling ball, her hat sailing in one direction, her legs and body flying in the other. She came to rest with a thud on the other side of the street beneath a Ford pickup, her left forearm snapped in two like a toothpick. The tail end of the easterly breeze caught the bottom of her dress and blew it up over her face. She lay unmoving, pointed downhill, her yellow dress now spotted red.

I got to her first, followed quickly by the lady behind the cash register, who was crazy-eyed and screaming uncontrollably. Within two seconds a crowd amassed.

Annie's eyes were closed, her frame limp, and her skin translucent and white. Her tongue had collapsed into her airway and was choking her, causing her face to turn blue while her body faded to sheet white. Unsure whether her spinal cord had sustained injury, I held her neck still and used my handkerchief to pull her tongue forward, clearing her airway and allowing her lungs to suck in air. I knew even the slightest movement of her neck risked further injury to her spine, if indeed her spine was injured, but I had to clear the airway. No air, no life. Given my options, I chose.

Martin moves the camera in a fluid ballet performance. First, it follows the breeze through town until it hits the lemonade stand, causing the fateful incident of Annie's money blowing into the street. Did you notice how then the camera turns and Pans to the delivery truck, angling on the driver and panning along as it crashes into Annie? Then, with a Close-Up, he brings us near enough to see Annie's condition, prodding both his protagonist and reader toward an emotional response.

Martin could have kept the camera on the sidewalk, only documenting the moment when the money blew into the street, and Annie running out and the truck hitting her. No doubt he could have written that just as beautifully. But by adding the cinematic effects he does, he elevates this scene enormously. The wind becomes not just a bit of weather but a key player. Did you notice how, with a touch of finality, the wind ends with a flip of Annie's dress so that it covers her face, much like the way a sheet will be pulled over a person's face who has just died? No doubt Martin used this image and element very deliberately. His protagonist is a doctor—one who wants to remain incognito, but now he has a choice and has to act, which will expose his well-kept secret. He has to save a little girl's life.

So when you are planning out your camera shots and envisioning your scenes, think about panning. Think of where you might start the camera rolling so as to build tension and show important details that will heighten the high moment you plan to spotlight in your scene. Think of specific elements in the setting that can be used as symbols or vehicles to evoke the kind of emotion you want to draw from your reader. Panning is a sure way to supercharge your novel.

Follow Along

Depending on the point of view and style of writing, moving shots can either seem like they are occurring inside the character's head in the way they view and interact with their world or appear as if we are watching the character in motion. *Follow* simply means what it implies: the camera follows the character in action. In a novel written in omniscient POV, the camera will often "follow" the characters and action as the story is told. In a novel using first-person point of view, writers can give a sense of "following" the character by moving along with them as they go about their business.

In the novel *The Fence My Father Built*, written by Linda S. Clare, we watch her protagonist, Muri, leaving the trailer she's staying in and heading on her way. While walking, we see the things she notices and thus learn more about her.

> I crept past Lutie, who sat planted in the green recliner with her basket of crochet yarns and what must have been a Bible. After a wave and a whispered explanation, I tiptoed outside.
>
> The air was still and almost icy; my eyes watered from its sting. During the night I'd awoken, shivering, not remembering at first where I was. I'd read somewhere that the desert temperature could go from a daytime sizzle to freezing after sundown, and now I didn't doubt it.

Across the yard the mound of bike parts glistened with the early morning wetness that I'd always heard was angel tears. Some of the sprockets stared at me, their gaping eyes rimmed with metal eyelashes. It could have been a postmodern sculpture. "In New York you'd fetch big bucks," I told it.

Walking would warm me. I crossed the rickety bridge that spanned the creek and started off toward the road to town. I pumped my arms, striding briskly along the rutted lane, where evergreens, withered and skeletal, blended into the gray green of the sage. Tiny had said the trees were infested with a kind of beetle, killing them an inch at a time. This saddened me and I walked faster.

The only colors came from the sunrise and the earth itself, reds and dusty pinks. I was careful to avoid little holes in the ground, which I imagined to be rattlesnake hideouts and tarantula dens. I reminded myself to leave them alone and they'll leave you alone. Still, a hawk's cry overhead startled me. A small rabbit darted back into the brush. I suspected the poor hare wouldn't get far with the "live and let be" attitude.

That philosophy didn't work as well with other areas of life, either, I'd discovered. For the last twenty-four hours I'd gone along with whatever came, tried not to judge, slept in the corner of a trailer that was so junked out it set my teeth on edge. Nova had immediately stuck her glow-in-the-dark plastic stars to our bedroom ceiling and their phosphorescence had only kept me awake.

I walked faster, no longer fighting off the urge to get this run-down place in shape.

Notice how much Clare reveals in this brief jaunt her character takes. We get a sense of a camera following her, all the while, in Muri's head, her own "camera" is Angling On details like the glistening bike parts. Her inner camera uses Long Shots and Close-Ups and even Follows the rabbit darting into the bush. In essence, we see the same scene being shot from within and without. Sounds confusing, but Clare does this seamlessly to great effect. We learn important things about her character as we follow her on her way.

In Jodi Picoult's novel *Nineteen* Minutes, about a school shooting, we follow Patrick, a police officer, who gets the report of the school shooting and runs inside a building looking for the shooter:

As he raced up the steps to the school, he was vaguely aware of two other patrol officers bucking the chief's commands and joining him in the fray. Patrick directed them each down a different hallway, and then he himself pushed through the double doors, past students who were shoving each other in an effort to get outside. Fire alarms blared so loudly that Patrick had to strain to hear the gunshots. He grabbed the coat of a boy streaking past him. "Who is it?" he yelled. "Who's shooting?"

The kid shook his head, speechless, and wrenched away. Patrick watched him run crazily down the hallway, open the door, burst into a rectangle of sunlight.

Students funneled around him, as if he were a stone in a river. Smoke billowed and burned his eyes. Patrick heard another staccato of gunshots and had to restrain himself from running toward them blindly. "How many of them?" he cried as a girl ran by.

"I . . . I don't know . . ."

The boy beside her turned around and looked at Patrick, torn between offering knowledge and getting the hell out of there. "It's a kid . . . he's shooting everyone . . ."

That was enough. Patrick pushed against the tide, a salmon swimming upstream. Homework papers were scattered on the floor; shell casings rolled beneath the heels of his shoes. Ceiling tiles had been shot off, and a fine gray dust coated the broken bodies that lay twisted on the floor. Patrick ignored all of this, going against most of his training—running past doors that might hide a perp, disregarding rooms that should have been searched— instead driving forward with his weapon drawn and his heart beating through every inch of his skin . . .

He pounded up the main stairwell, and just as he reached the top, a door cracked open. Patrick whirled, pointing his gun, as a young female teacher fell to her knees with her hands raised. Behind the while oval of her face were twelve others, featureless and frightened.

He continues to run through the school, into the gym, seeing more bodies, hearing more shots, and the camera follows along with him. Finally, he finds a boy shivering in the corner of the locker room.

"Are you okay?" Patrick whispered. He did not want to speak

out loud and give away his position to the shooter.

The boy only blinked at him.

"Where is he?" Patrick mouthed.

The boy pulled a pistol from beneath his thigh and held it up to his own head.

And then we watch what happens after Patrick realizes this boy is the killer he's been hunting. As the camera follows Patrick through the rooms and corridors of the school, Patrick's "inner camera" is angling on things, zooming up close as he notices clues like shell casings, the papers scattered across the floor, and the dust on the bodies he encounters.

So think about the scenes in which your character is moving from one place to another and how you can "follow" him and see what he is doing, all the while staying inside his head and seeing and noticing what he sees. What he notices and how he reacts reveals character just as importantly—and maybe even more so—as watching your character from *outside* his head and seeing what he's up to, plot-wise. As tricky as it sounds, a good novelist will master this very useful cinematic tool, and you can too.

Chapter 11

Seeing through the Character's Eyes

POV Shot

Novelists are very familiar with the term POV, which stands for point of view. Whether only one point of view is used throughout a novel or many, every scene in a novel has to be in some point of view. In first-person POV, the camera is always in one character's head, and the story is told through her and watching her as the plot plays on. With third-person POV, the camera may move from character to character, but can only be in one person's "head" at a time—whoever is the POV character for the scene.

Using an omniscient third-person POV gives an author a little more leeway to flit in and out of many characters' heads and know things the characters may have no clue of. The omniscient storyteller is akin to a god who knows and sees all, but tells only what he chooses. The scope of a novelist's creativity is bound and determined by POV.

A movie, for the most part, takes on the role of omniscient storyteller. Sometimes you'll come across a story that is being told by a character whom we don't see directly speaking but addresses the viewer (called Voice Over, or V. O. in a screenplay—see the excerpt below).

For example, in the screenplay *The Shawshank Redemption* (written by Frank Darabont and based on a story by Stephen King) near the beginning of the movie, after we see the protagonist Andy Defresne convicted (wrongly) of murdering his wife and being ordered to serve two life sentences, we are introduced to Red (played by Morgan Freeman), a man who's been in the clink for twenty years. We see him briefly before the parole board attesting to his rehabilitation, followed by a Close-Up of his parole form being stamped in red ink with the large word *Rejected*. Then we hear the voice of Red speaking from "offstage," and we understand now the movie is going to be told from his point of view.

RED emerges into fading daylight, slouches low-key through the activity, worn cap on his head, exchanging hellos and doing minor business. He's an important man here.

                    RED (V.O.)
     There's a con like me in every
     prison in America, I guess. I'm the
     guy who can get it for you.
     Cigarettes, a bag of reefer if
     you're partial, a bottle of brandy
     to celebrate your kid's high school
     graduation. Damn near anything,
     within reason.

He slips somebody a pack of smokes, smooth sleight of hand.

                    RED (V.O.)
     Yes sir, I'm a regular Sears &
     Roebuck.

TWO SHORT SIREN BLASTS issue from the main tower, drawing everybody's attention to the loading dock. The outer gate swings open ...revealing a gray prison bus outside.

                    RED (V.O.)
     So when Andy Dufresne came to me in
     1949 and asked me to smuggle Rita
     Hayworth into the prison for him, I
     told him no problem. And it wasn't.

In a movie like *The Shawshank Redemption*, you have the equivalent, roughly, of a first-person story. Of course, there are many scenes Red is not in, such as the great scene in which his buddy Andy locks himself in the warden's office and blasts opera through the loudspeakers into the yard. And the scenes in which Andy escapes. Yet, often we hear Red's voice telling what Andy did, at least at the beginning of such a scene, giving the impression that what we're seeing on the screen is still being told by Red.

In a film like this, being told clearly from some point way in the future, the storyteller can relate the account of what happened with an omniscient POV.

The Camera as a POV Character

Other movies that don't use this type of structure use the camera as the POV. Instead of using one character to tell the story, the camera is the observer and recorder of events, and a camera has no feelings, emotions, subjective thoughts, interpretations, or commentary. This is important to understand when discussing the camera shot POV. Here, for instance, is a POV shot from *The Fugitive*:

Gerard continues after Kimble.

The helicopter circles and follows from above.

INT. PENTHOUSE / DOOR TO ROOF - NIGHT

Renfro triggers his radio.

                    RENFRO
          There is a U.S. Marshal out there.
          Hold your fire!

HELICOPTER'S POV

FOLLOWING Kimble. Its beam tracking Kimble across the rooftop. He moves through the blowers and duct work. Kimble is gaining ground on Nichols.

```
ON SHARPSHOOTER

He is about to fire when he hears through his
radio.

                    RADIO (V.O.)
               Hold your fire.

The shooter pulls back.
```

Surely a helicopter can't emote or ponder what is going on, but in a movie, it can have a POV.

POV—Anything but Subjective

In a screenplay, when a POV shot is specified, the writer is instructing this segment of film to be shot as if looking through the eyes of a particular character (or object, as we saw in the excerpt above). Sound familiar? It's exactly what novelists do all the time. But there's a difference.

Remember, the camera has no thoughts or feelings; it only observes and records. It's a way of shifting what the camera is seeing, but it's *not* subjective. It's wholly objective. And this, for most novelists, is a bit foreign. For, POV and subjectivity seem to go hand in hand, right? Not in screenplays.

Using the camera shot POV is a great technique novelists can imitate. For some writers, the idea of showing a scene completely devoid of emotion, reaction, internalizing, and opining may seem counterintuitive—or downright counterproductive. Isn't the whole point to tell a story up close and personal?

Sure. But there may be times when you want to see action happening without coloring it with any subjective tint. When you want a feeling of emotional distance. Some writers excel in this technique, and their novels become a visual palette of story shown as if through an impersonal camera. The effect is often profound and evocative. Why? Because it is left to the reader entirely to come up with what isn't shown or told, to assess the emotional content and intention of the characters and the story unfolding.

Perhaps one of the best among contemporary writers at using the POV shot is Cormac McCarthy, who won the Pulitzer for his post-apocalyptic novel *The Road*. I've read most of McCarthy's novels, but I have to admit that when I first opened *All the Pretty Horses*, I got so frustrated by his impersonal style and run-on sentences that I almost gave up. At first it really irritated me, but then, after I allowed myself to go with the flow of his writing style and follow his "camera," I became enthralled. It took some getting used to, and I don't know if many writers can pull it off the way he can and still engage readers and make them care for his characters, but he makes it work.

Here are two short paragraph excerpts as examples—the first from *The Road* and the second from *Cities of the Plain*. Note the impersonality of the description as he uses the POV shot.

When he got back the boy was still asleep. He pulled the blue plastic tarp off him and folded it and carried it out to the grocery cart and packed it and came back with their plates and some cornmeal cakes in a plastic bag and a plastic bottle of syrup. He spread the small tarp they used for a table on the ground and laid everything out and he took the pistol from his belt and laid it on the cloth and then he just sat watching the boy sleep.

~~~

It was late when he got back but the light was still on in the kitchen. He sat in the truck for a minute, then he shut off the engine. He left the key in the ignition and got out and walked across the yard to the house. Socorro had gone to bed but there was cornbread in the warmer over the oven and a plate of beans and potatoes with two pieces of fried chicken. He carried the plates to the table and went back and got silver out of the dish drainer and got down a cup and poured his coffee and set the pot back over the eye of the stove where there was still a dull red glow of coals and he took his coffee to the table and sat and ate. He ate slowly and methodically. When he'd finished he carried the dishes to the sink and opened the refrigerator and bent to scout the interior for anything in the way of dessert. He found a bowl of pudding and took it to the sideboard and got down a small dish and filled it and put the pudding back in the refrigerator and got more coffee and sat eating the pudding and reading Oren's newspaper. The clock ticked in the hallway. The cooling stove creaked. When John Grady came in he went on to the stove and got a cup of coffee and came to the table and sat down and pushed back his hat.

By using this POV shot, McCarthy just shows the bare bones of action with commentary, thereby inviting the reader to supply her own. At first glance, it may appear to be boring narrative. But the result of this technique is a masterful picture of era, locale, and, yes, character. For the things we do reveal much about who we are. POV shots are the ultimate "show, don't tell."

Of course, writers don't have to write entire novels in this style or solely using a POV camera angle. There may be a scene here and there in which this might be the perfect camera shot. Maybe you are writing a mystery and you want to show a sequence of events happening but don't want to clue the reader in on the importance of what is being seen. Or, for that matter, perhaps not even on *whose* point of view the camera is seeing from. You see this on occasion in suspense thrillers as a scene is experienced through the POV of the undetermined killer.

Preparing to Put It All Together

We've now gone through the basic stationary and moving camera shots. You have an idea of what each shot is and how it might be used in a screenplay or novel. But as you know, no movie or novel is "shot" using just one camera angle. Each scene needs to be planned out and the best shots chosen for greatest impact.

Remember, the goal is to lead to the high moment of each scene, and it will take a number of shots to get there, and some shots often will follow after that high moment as well. Filmmakers will sometimes "storyboard," which means they actually sketch out frames of images implying which shot will be used when, how, and focusing on what. If you're good at drawing or can even manage a few stick figures, you could try laying out your scenes on big pieces of poster board. But you can also jot down camera shots in a list, playing around with them until you have a sequence that will meet your needs.

Whatever method you use, know you now have your writer's toolbox filled with all kinds of neat camera shots you can use to shoot your novel. So let's take a look at how some successful novelists do just that.

Part 3

Orchestrating the Symphony of Shots

Combining Camera Angles for the Greatest Effect

We've spent much time going over camera shots, looking at various stationary and moving shots used in screenplays. You've now seen how each particular shot can be transcribed effectively in a novel, and hopefully you now have some great tools that you can use to supercharge your novel and make it visually powerful.

Using a camera shot in a scene will do much to bring it alive for the reader, but as in movies, novel scenes are made up of segments, a string of moments that may include various movements, internal thoughts, gestures and expressions, dialog, all leading up to the high moment in each scene. The fine arts of movie directing and film editing come into play as the novelist pulls together all the needed shots to create a dynamic scene that packs a punch. Novelists become orchestra conductors, drawing upon an entire symphony of "instruments" to enthrall their readers with a beautiful composition.

So let's take a look at some examples of scenes in which writers effectively use a combination of shots in order to lead readers to the emotional places they want them to go. A skilled writer will choose each segment shot deliberately, pointing out exactly what he wants his readers to notice and pay attention to, in order to move the plot along, set the pacing and tension, and bond them with his characters. When done well, the result is a powerful novel whose imagery will be burned into memory for a long time. For, images—more than words or abstract concepts—stick the longest.

It's said the expression "a picture paints a thousand words" comes from this ancient Chinese saying: "One showing is better than one hundred sayings." When novelists show instead of tell—and show using powerful cinematic technique—they will see the truth in this saying.

Chapter 12

Putting It All Together

Now that you've learned the various shots screenwriters use to piece together the segments in their movie scenes, let's take a look at a number of novel segments from books written by best-selling authors. No doubt these authors have met with success due in part to their cinematic technique in writing. Some may utilize camera shots quite intuitively, and I doubt many, if any, actually lay out their scenes with a list of camera shots breaking the scenes down into the kind of pieces a screenwriter would. I don't doubt that novelists who are also screenwriters do this consciously on some level—even if only seeing the scene filmed in their head.

As I mentioned early on, we are so used to watching movies and TV that we automatically use camera shots without thinking. But my goal is to wrest you from the haphazard method of winging it and get you to plan ahead the way a director will. To think about your high moment of each scene and what that should look like.

And once you know what shot you will need in order to show that moment, you can design the rest of the scene around it. Now that you have all these tools in your writer's toolbox, you can pick and choose, play with the scene structure, and even try writing a scene a few different ways.

A Personal Example

To give you a personal example, here's what I thought about while I was writing my fantasy novel *The Crystal Scepter*, which is a fanciful retelling of the Greek legend of Perseus and Medusa. I had a key scene to write—the final scene of Part One, in which a lowly fisherman, on the sad anniversary of his son's drowning, goes outside the morning after a terrible storm to check his nets.

I knew well what the high moment of the scene would be: Arnyl finding a trunk tangled in his nets, and a baby, alive, inside the trunk. I knew this had to be a "big screen moment," as it is the pivotal plot element the entire book hinges on. The baby grows up to be the hero of the story, unknowing of his true royal parentage. So I wanted to build to this key moment both visually and emotionally.

I considered starting the scene with a Close-Up on Arnyl's hands as he tries to untangle the mess of nets in the cove by his beachside cottage. I thought I might then Pull Back and show the cove in a brief Establishing Shot. This way I could dive right into his frustration, show the storm-littered beach, have his grief compounded by this task. This could lead nicely into his finding the trunk and pulling it out.

Then I considered other factors. I wanted to get a little bit of backstory in about how his son drowned, and rather than have him just sit there thinking about what day it was, I wanted the scene more active. It is also the very first time you meet Arnyl, so I decided it would work better to show him stepping outside his cottage that morning and walking to the memorial stone he erected for his son. That way I could reveal his emotional state and tell a bit of the story, in his POV, of his guilt over the drowning, his drinking, his railing at heaven and himself.

Then I have the camera follow him as he Pans the beach with his gaze. And as he sees all the fish in his nets and starts filling up his cart, I slowly zoom in to a Close-Up, then Angle On the bit of trunk he spots bobbing in the water. The rest of the shot is a Close-Up to an Extreme Close-Up as he hefts the trunk onto the rocks, opens it, finds the baby, and then the note and the bag of gems underneath.

By making this the *only* Close-Up shot in the scene, it emphasizes the importance of what is seen. The reader is told: "Pay attention to these details—they're important."

Once Arnyl recovers from his shock and goes through the emotional upheaval of the realization heaven has sent him another son to raise, we Pull Back and see him head away from the cove, determined, changed, and with a plan. The literal Pull Back does a nice job of paralleling the emotional and mental Pull Back Arnyl does as he realizes his life has suddenly changed.

Does this seem like a whole lot of work? Maybe. But actually, this kind of cinematic planning makes writing the scene much easier than just winging it, or keeping the "camera" in one spot, even if you intend to "show" the scene in active, present action. Can you see how much more interesting and dynamic using this variety of specific, well-intentioned camera shots showcases the purpose and the high moment of the scene in a terrific way—and much more effectively than if the camera is just documenting what happens from one location on the "set"?

I hope this gives you an idea of how you can think through your scenes as you start piecing the plot of your book together. If you start with knowing the point or high moment of each scene—what important piece or plot or character reveal you plan to show—you can play with these different segments to determine just where and how to start off your scene, and how and with what camera shots to follow it through and build to that high moment.

It's not rocket science, and there's not just one way to do it. The fun is in the choice, and once you realize you can direct your scenes the way a movie director might, it opens up many exciting possibilities.

I hope you've been getting excited, because I do—every time I begin to think how to construct a scene in my novel. I don't just wing it or point and shoot randomly; I lay out a shooting schedule! May you find similar joy in wearing your screenwriter's hat too.

Let's Take a Look at Some Novel Scenes

Here's the opening scene from Lisa Gardner's thriller *Alone*. She uses cinematic technique throughout, adeptly choosing just the right camera shot to grab us and take us for a dynamically visual ride. Right away we get in her character's head and see what he sees, notice what he notices. His internal camera is on, seeing images in his head as the scene plays out.

I'll put in brackets the camera shots she uses to help you identify them.

He'd put in a fifteen-hour shift the night the call came in. Too many impatient drivers on 93, leading to too much crash, bang, boom. City was like that this time of year. The trees were bare, night coming on quick and the holidays looming. It felt raw outside. After the easy camaraderie of summer barbecues, you now walked alone through city streets hearing nothing but the skeletal rattle of dry leaves skittering across cold pavement. **[Establishing Shot]**

Lots of cops complained about the short, gray days of February, but personally, Bobby Dodge had never cared for November. Today did nothing to change his mind.

His shift started with a minor fender bender, followed by two more rear-enders from northbound gawkers. Four hours of paperwork later, he thought he'd gotten through the worst of it. **[Montage]** Then, in early afternoon, when traffic should've been a breeze even on the notoriously jam-packed 93, came a five-car pile-up as a speeding taxi driver tried to change four lanes at once and a stressed-out ad exec in a Hummer forcefully cut him off. The Hummer took the hit like a heavyweight champ. The rusted-out cab went down for the count and took out three other cars with it. Bobby got to call four wreckers, then diagram the accident, and then arrest the ad exec when it became clear the man had mixed in a few martinis with his power lunch. . . . **[Series of Shots]**

The mad grabbed the doorjamb with his right hand. He swung his lumbering body backwards, expecting to bowl over his smaller escort and what? **[Close-Up]** Make a run for it through a police barracks swarming with armed troopers? Bobby ducked left, struck out his foot, and watched the overweight executive slam to the floor. **[Two Shot]** The man landed with an impressive crash and a few troopers paused long enough to clap their hands at the free show. **[Full Shot]**

After playing out some of the dialog between the drunken exec and her protagonist, Gardner had Bobby head to the local bar, thinking he's done with work for the night. We see a Full Shot in which he's sitting with his buddies watching news on the mounted TV screen, which shows a hostage situation developing and the SWAT team coming in. Bobby's beeper then goes off, which sends him bolting out the door. She's used great camera technique to set her hero up in his ordinary world, establishing his vocation and personality, then moves right into the premise of the novel and introducing a first major incident.

By using the various camera shots to give a feel for Bobby's work and the kind of day he's had, Gardener brings the scene to life. She focuses on just a few things in the three scant pages of her opening scene, but it tells us a lot about her protagonist by showing him in action and seeing what he sees—not just around him but what's playing in his head. He thinks about the crazy events of the day, using a Montage and Series of Shots. And we watch one piece of that day played up more up close and personal. The variety of shots helps with interest, pacing, and tension.

In the next chapter, we see Bobby now heading toward that hostage situation and realize he's been appointed the sniper-shooter. Watch as Gardner has the camera Pan and Follow him through the streets of Boston.

Roaring through the streets of Boston, he squealed his tires taking a hard right up Park Street, heading for the golden-domed State House, then threw his cruiser left onto Beacon, flying past the Common and the Public Garden. At the last minute, he almost blew it—tried to head up Arlington straight for Marlborough, then realized that Marlborough was one way the wrong way. Like any good Masshole driver, he slammed on his brakes, cranked the wheel hard, and laid on his horn as he sliced across three lanes of traffic to stay off Beacon. Now his life was tougher, trying to pick up the right cross street to head up to Marlborough. In the end, he simply drove toward the white glow of floodlights and the flashing red lights of the Advanced Life Support ambulance.

Arriving at the corner of Marlborough and Gloucester, Bobby processed many details at once. Blue sawhorses and Boston PD cruisers already isolated one tiny block in the heart of Back Bay. **[Long Shot]** Yellow crime-scene tape festooned several brownstone houses, and uniformed officers were taking up position on the corners. The ALS ambulance was now on-scene; so were several vans from the local media. **[Pan to see all this]**

Things were definitely starting to rock and roll.

Bobby double-parked his Crown Vic just outside a blue sawhorse, jumped out the door, and jogged around to his trunk. **[Follow]** Inside he had everything a well-trained police sniper might need for a party. Rifle scope ammo, black BDUs, urban came BDUs, ghillie hood, body armor, changes of clothing, snacks, water, a bean bag, night-vision goggles, binoculars, range finder, face paint, Swiss Army knife, and flashlight. **[Close-Up]**

After Bobby assesses the situation, gears up, and finds the ideal place to set up his position, he approaches the old brownstone building and finds a man there who refused to heed the evacuation order. In a Two Shot, we watch Bobby talk to the man and ask how to get to the top floor, and the man happily shows him the way. His gaze Pans the room, taking in the furnishings, then he sets up his equipment and weapons. Using binoculars, he Angles On the suspect he's been told to single out, then positions his rifle and looks through the crosshairs at his target. After some time, the suspect moves, and Bobby's "camera" Finds and Zooms in on a woman kneeling by the bed and a small child. It's a Long Shot, and he can't see much detail from where he sits.

Through the scope he Zooms in and Zooms out, and he can tell the man's yelling, but in this Long Shot he's too far away to hear anything. But once he can tell the child's out of the way, and the man is about to pull the trigger on the handgun he's holding to his wife's head [Angle On the finger on the trigger], Bobby does what he came to do. He shoots. All very cinematic.

Ending the Scene on the High Moment

In James Patterson's novel *Kill Me If You Can*, an art student finds a bag of diamonds during an attack at New York's Grand Central Station. Matthew Bannon recounts that night.

> When the post-rush hour lull at Grand Central is shattered by gunshots and followed by two loud explosions, only one thing comes to mind.
> *Terrorist Attack.*
> In an instant, the collective paranoia was justified. Mass panic ensued.
> The screams echoed off the walls of the marble cavern. The first thing I saw was that nobody ducked for cover. Everybody ran—with visions of the crumbling towers replaying in their heads, I'm sure. **[Long Shot, maybe a Pan seeing people running]**
> And then I couldn't see a thing. Red smoke filled the building
> . . .
> I ran like the rest of them.
> And then I saw it in the smoky haze.
> A trail of blood. **[Angle On]**

Instinctively I followed it. And then I saw him. **[Follows, Finds]**

He was a big bear of a man, slumped against a bank of lockers in a pool of his own blood—from a gaping wound in his neck. **[Full Shot]**

In all the madness, nobody was paying any attention to him. I knelt at his side. **[Two Shot]**

My knee hit something hard. A gun. **[Insert, in his mind]**

"Get doctor. Stop blood." He gurgled out the words in a thick Russian accent.

But there was no time for a doctor. No time for anything.

Before I could say a word, his eyes rolled back in his head and he exhaled a strained breath. He was dead. **[Close-Up]**

His dark blue suit and the floor around him glistened with blood. **[Pull Back]** It coated the door of the bottom locker closest to him. As I looked up, I saw a wide swath of red where he had leaned against the upper locker and slid to the ground. **[Pan]**

Locker #925 was covered in bloody handprints. **[Angle On or Finds in a Close-Up]**

And it was open.

Wide open.

Patterson leaves the reader hanging, wondering just what is in that locker (although the inside jacket flaps tells what's in there). Still, the scene moves at a fast pace with the succinct writing and lots of perfect camera angles.

Patterson only includes the details we need to see to keep the tension up and the action moving. He could have added more description of the station, the people around Bannon, the smells and sounds, but Patterson writes with a sparse commercial style. The scene would still be dynamic and powerful with more added.

What makes it work, though, is his choice of camera angles. He doesn't just "tell" what happens; he shows very specifically, making the reader see what he wants him to see. He follows his character, and the reader follows Bannon's gaze as he takes in the pandemonium around him, spots the blood trail, finds the dying man, then—to punch in the high moment of the scene—rivets his attention on one particular wide-open locker, which no doubt gives a glimpse of what's inside. Well done indeed.

Combining Shots to Skew Time and Perception

In Don DeLillo's novel *Falling Man* (2007), we are thrust into the story just after the first NY Trade Tower has crumpled to the ground. In a wonderfully creative and potent narrative, DeLillo uses a variety of camera shots to evoke the chaos both within and without.

It was not a street anymore but a world, a time and space of falling ash and near night. **[Establishing Shot]** He was walking north through rubble and mud and there were people running past holding towels to their faces or jackets over their heads. They had handkerchiefs pressed to their mouths. They had shoes in their hands, a woman with a shoe in each hand, running past him. They ran and fell, some of them, confused and ungainly, with debris coming down around them, and there were people taking shelter under cars. **[Pan from his POV]**

The roar was still in the air, the buckling rumble of the fall. This was the world now. Smoke and ash came rolling down streets and turning corners, busting around corners, seismic tides of smoke, with office paper flashing past, standard sheets with cutting edge, skimming whipping past, otherworldly things in the morning pall. **[Continued Pan]**

He wore a suit and carried a briefcase. There was glass in his hair and face, marbled bolls of blood and light. **[Full Shot but out of his POV]** He walked past a Breakfast Special sign and they went running by, city cops and security guards running, hands pressed down on gun butts to keep the weapons steady.

[Montage] Things inside were distant and still, where he was supposed to be. It happened everywhere around him, a car half buried in debris, windows smashed and noises coming out, radio voices scratching at the wreckage. He saw people shedding water as they ran, clothes and bodies drenched from sprinkler systems. There were shoes discarded in the street, handbags and laptops, a man seated on the sidewalk coughing up blood. Paper cups went bouncing oddly by.

The world was this as well, figures in windows a thousand feet up, dropping into free space, and the stink of fuel fire, and the steady rip of sirens in the air. The noise lay everywhere they ran, stratified sound collecting around them, and he walked away from it and into it at the same time.

There was something else then, outside all this, not belonging to this, aloft. He watched it coming down. A shirt came down out of the high smoke, a shirt lifted and drifting in the scant light and then falling again, down toward the river. **[Angle On]**

DeLillo does a magnificent job of narrative with the overlapping and repeating words, giving the sense of muddled confusion for his character. And the way the camera Pans and catches on random visuals (as well as other sensory things like sounds) heightens the horror of this moment. Much of the narrative is with a POV shot—without emotion or commentary. And we get just a quick Full Shot of his character emphasizing only the bits of blood in his hair. By having this man's eyes catch on the drifting shirt—lingering longer on this image than the others—DeLillo gives the sense of time slowing.

The reader can imagine stopping and gazing, shocked by the mayhem around him, absently glued to this piece of cloth as it slowly floats to earth. This, in contrast to what he noted a few sentences earlier about those who were falling from the top floors of the tower—again detached emotionally.

Why does he do this—remove the emotion from the equation? Writers are told to have their characters react. But his unnamed character (who could be any man anywhere), is too stunned to react at all.

The Angle On the shirt emphasizes its symbolism as it's brought to the forefront of all these colliding images. Why is this one thing—out of all the debris falling around him—not belonging? What does it say about this character? We are not told, but we get a sense of significance by the attention put on it.

A Variety of Shots to Paint the Big Picture

Here's a great sequence of shots from the opening of *Apocalypse Now* (1975) showing the camera moving in and out, panning, making the viewer see a series of specific things writer/director Francis Ford Coppola feels it's important to see (the original screenplay was written by John Milius).

Coppola's aim is to get close and personal to the experience of being in this primal jungle in a hotbed of war, practically immersing the viewer in the swamp of mud.

PRIMEVAL SWAMP - EARLY DAWN

It is very early in the dawn - blue light
filters through the jungle and across a foul
swamp. A mist clings to the trees. This could
be the jungle of a million years ago.

Our VIEW MOVES CLOSER, through the mist,
TILTING DOWN to the tepid water. A small
bubble rises to the surface; then another.
Suddenly, but quietly, a form begins to
emerge; a helmet. Water and mud pour off
revealing a set of beady eyes just above the
mud. Printed on a helmet, in a psychedelic
hand, are the words: "Gook Killer." The head
emerges revealing that the tough-looking
soldier beneath has exceptionally long hair
and beard; he has no shirt on, only bandoliers
of ammunition - his body is
painted in an odd camouflage pattern. He looks
to the right; he looks to the left; he looks
INTO CAMERA, and slowly sinks back into the
swamp, disappearing completely.

Our VIEW HOLDS, We begin to HEAR natural,
though unrecognizable, JUNGLE SOUNDS, far off
in the distance.
We PAN TO REVEAL a clump of logs half
submerged in the Swamp, and part of what seems
to be a Falstaff beer can in the mud. A hand
reaches out, and the beer can disappears.

As we TILT UP, we NOTICE that the log is
hollow and houses the rear of an M-60 machine
gun, hand painted in a paisley design.

Now the VIEW MOVES AWAY, ACROSS the ancient
growth, PAST the glimmer of what seems to be
another soldier hiding in ambush, wearing an
exotic hat made from birds and bushes. ACROSS
to a dark trail where the legs of those in
black pajamas move silently across our ever

```
TIGHTENING   VIEW.  Their   feet,   boots,   and
sandals leave no impression, make
no sound. A slight flicker of light reveals a
pair of eyes in the foliage across the path,
waiting and watching.

The VIEW PUSHES ALONG WITH the Vietnamese,
MOVING FASTER AND FASTER WITH them, until
suddenly,  directly  in  front  about  ten  feet
away, an enormous AMERICAN, clad in rags
and bushes and holding a 12 gauge automatic
shotgun casually at his side, steps in front
of them. He smiles laconically and BLASTS OUT
FIVE SHOTS that rip THROUGH US. By the second
shot, the whole jungle blazes out
with AUTOMATIC FIRE.
```

I hope you're beginning to understand how screenwriters "put it all together" by stringing together segments of various shots, creating visually dynamic scenes that powerfully lead to a high moment and evoke emotional reaction. And now you are seeing how novelists can do the very same thing—with similar results. By studying successful novelists who use cinematic technique in their writing, you can become adept at this transference of camera shots and supercharge your story.

When you read a particularly moving or riveting scene in a novel, stop and examine which camera shots are being used. Think how you might film this scene, and take a look at the high moment punctuated by a particular camera shot.

If you are reading a novel and struggling to get through a boring, flat scene, ask yourself these questions:

- How could I rewrite this scene using camera shots to make it more intriguing and visually exciting?

- What is the high moment (if any), and how could it be better enhanced by a particular camera shot?

- If there isn't a high moment, is there something that does happen in the scene that could become the high point (advancing the plot or revealing character), and what does that look like?

- Are there any camera shots being used? How many? Could there be more or better ones? Which ones?

- Is the camera just stuck in one place? If so, what key moment in the dialog or action needs to be emphasized, and which camera shot would be best to use?

No doubt you can see where I'm going with this, for these should be the very questions you are asking about *your* novel's scenes.

Do Your Homework

Take the time to study great novels that have cinematic power, but also take a look at novel scenes that have no punch—or point to them. As a reader, you know what rivets your attention, what chokes you up or moves you to tears. You probably have favorite novels and can tell anyone what your favorite scene or moment is in those novels. All I have to do is start relating what happens at the end of *The Art of Racing in the Rain* and I start crying. In fact, when my editor from my publishing house got into a discussion with me about this great book and the moving ending, we both started crying—dog lovers that we are. Wouldn't it be great if your novel was one that others couldn't stop talking about?

By using cinematic technique, you can turn a good novel into a great one. You too can create emotionally charged scenes. So when you sit down to plot out or write your scenes, rummage through your writer's toolbox and consciously use these different shots to supercharge your story.

But There's More!

As you've seen, movies are made up of numerous camera shots. But that is not all there is to cinematic technique—far from it. Filmmakers have to take so much more into consideration when planning and shooting their movie.

Ever pay close attention to the list of credits at the end of a movie—especially a high-budget epic action-adventure movie? The list of credits runs on and on and on. And you see people's names listed with strange titles like foley artist, greensman, gaffer, grip, and colorist. Many people are needed to focus on just one aspect of a film, such as sound, music, lighting, or special effects. And I'm sure fiction writers could learn some insightful techniques from every one of them.

However, rather than go into every little bit of film technique novelists might benefit from (which could fill volumes), I'm going to ask you to wear just a few more hats. Seeing your novel with a filmmaker's eye can open up new vistas and ways of portraying your story beyond just the camera shot. So let's go "behind the scenes" and take a look at this cinematic world.

Chapter 13

Using a Filmmaker's Eye

Designing Shots for Subconscious Effect

Filmmakers are concerned with the design of shots. They are artists with a creative sense of composition, and their aim is to arrange their compositions in ways that will evoke emotional reactions from the viewer. The movie screen is their palette with which they paint visual pictures, and the "colors" on their palette are the various camera shots they choose from to create the perfect effect they hope to achieve in each segment they shoot.

In addition to using specific lenses, they consider lighting, the positioning of the camera for subliminal or subconscious effect, shapes and colors that lend toward thematic and symbolic imagery, music and sound effects to enhance the desired mood, and special effects like lens distortion or the speeding up or slowing down of the shot to tweak the sense of time passing. So many factors come into play in creating a beautifully composed segment or scene. And novelists can learn much from the way filmmakers deftly utilize all these components.

Making Shots Resonate

Why do certain shots resonate with us when we watch movies? Have you ever been awed by a special moment in a film—not because of the plot or the acting but due to the visual impact of the composition before you? Often this happens at the "high moment" of the scene, when the camera pulls back and we're shown something profound, or it may be due to the combination of elements and colors that a deep poignancy has been conveyed. I think of movies like *Hero* and *Crouching Tiger, Hidden Dragon* with their gorgeous scenes drenched in color that go deep into symbolism and evoke emotion, enhancing the action shown on the screen.

Gustav Mercado discusses the film *Up in the Air* in his book *The Filmmaker's Eye*. He tells how he and some friends discussed the movie after seeing it, and they noticed they had all been struck by a particular moment in the movie. A character named Natalie is sitting in an empty room full of chairs after a number of employees have been fired (which she was partly responsible for). The composition itself is symbolic, the filmmaker doing more than just using a simple Wide Shot to create effect. Here are some of the things these viewers noticed about the composition of the shot:

- Having her be the only person in a room full of empty chairs emphasizes the scope of the "damage" done (the large number of people fired).

- The shot is taken from an elevated angle, looking down on her, which makes her seem small and lonely. The emotional effect of this angle "makes her look defeated, vulnerable, and distraught."

- The high angle allows the viewer to see all the chairs (whereas if the shot had been taken at eye level, many of the chairs' backs would block the others and Natalie.

- The chairs are mostly facing in a way that seems as if they are pushing her into the corner, physically and emotionally. This works as subtext against what she says when she's picked up by her friend (implying she's fine, when she's not).

Every Aspect of a Scene Should Enhance Story

Gustav Mercado says, "This comprehensive and integrated conceptualization of every shot in your film is essential to truly harness the power of this art form and connect with the audience. . . . You want to create compositions that reflect meaningful aspects of your story. You need to think about your story in a cinematic way, to create shot compositions that visually emphasize significant plot details, as well as its themes, motifs, and core ideas."

Wow, this is a tall order. And novelists, like filmmakers, should have a similar vision for their work. That is, if they really want to create powerful, moving stories that excite readers. There is so much more to telling a story than just, well, telling it. Or even showing it. By putting on your filmmaker's hat you can extend and enrich your technique to include the cinematic secrets great filmmakers know about and use very consciously. Knowing all these camera shots that we've gone over is the first step. But there is so much more. And the first and foremost item of importance is really knowing your story.

Get a Clear Vision

Mercado says, "If you want to become an effective storyteller, one of the most important things you can do is to have a clear vision of your story, so that it reflects your unique take on it, not somebody else's. . . . Anything and everything that is included in the composition of a shot will be interpreted by an audience as being there for a specific purpose that is directly related and necessary to understand the story they are watching [or reading, in the case of a novel]."

Writers, as well as filmmakers, need to first identify the core ideas of their story in order to create what's called an image system. Once that is determined, they can design a system that supports and brings out that core idea in either obvious or subtle ways consistently implemented throughout the book.

So before you choose which "shot" you will use for a particular segment of your scene, ask these questions:

- What are the main elements (or one main element) that should dominate the scene and be brought to the reader's attention?

- What should and shouldn't be included in the shot?

- What meaning will be conveyed by the shot *subconsciously*?

Of course, this is all in relation to that high moment you are striving for. And overlaying all this is your main theme or core idea. You've perhaps been told you should be able to sum up your premise in a sentence or two (elevator pitch). In that premise lies your core idea for your book. You may have gotten a germ of an idea for your novel, and from that you developed characters with issues and goals, and you came up with settings and scene ideas to play out your storyline. But overlaying all that is your *core idea*. And that's where the decisions about scene compositions come in.

In Just a Few Words

See if you can encapsulate the main theme or idea of your story in one line or a few words. For example, the core idea behind the movie *Rocky* might be about gaining self-respect. That's a simple summation. But if you can come up with a basic thematic concept, you can gear all your shots and special effects to bring out that theme.

All the angles used; the colors, shapes, and sounds layered; and the special effects (tweaked time, distorted lenses, etc.) can all be selected to enhance that theme. Using visual motifs and symbols repeatedly through a novel press home the themes in a powerful way. Many novelists do this already, but understanding some of the cinematic secrets filmmakers use will give the writer a few more useful tools in that writer's toolbox.

Mercado claims that "every shot counts, no matter how inconsequential (and no shot should be inconsequential in the first place since it is included in your film, right?)" Do you consider every segment of every scene in your novel important? Is it worth it to you to design each scene so that it nurtures your themes? Do you feel every word counts and should count?

If you approach the art of novel writing in a manner similar to a filmmaker like Mercado, you will take the time to set up your shots and effects such that they will supercharge the story you are trying to tell.

Going beyond the Choice of Camera Shot

I mentioned that filmmakers use a term called "image systems." Novelists can learn much from this. Image systems include repeating shot compositions—for example, a movie might use a certain shape or image in a landscape and repeat it throughout the film. An image system often uses specific colors—some which may not be easy at first to notice, and that work on a subliminal level in some way.

Great novelists know the power of motif and symbolism, often using something like a repeated word or phrase, or an object of importance to the character, to bring a richness to the story and to enhance the theme of their novel. In effect, they are creating something similar to an image system. By taking a look at some of the ways filmmakers develop image systems for their films, novelists can learn much and expand their technique.

Elements Used in Image Systems

In the movie *The Sixth Sense*, writer/director Shyamalan uses red to link with the supernatural. In every scene in which something "beyond the veil" is shown, you'll find an object in red: a balloon, a sweater, a tent, and many others. Using a repeated color is probably the most common element in an image system.

But there are other things that can act as symbols or motifs in a visual image system. In *K-Pax* (2001)—a movie whose premise centers on traveling on light beams—in many of the scenes light is captured and portrayed in a creative evocative way, consciously and unconsciously reminding the viewer that light is the element tying the entire story together, as well as acting as symbol on many levels. Prot, the protagonist not only travels on light, he is what the pure essence of light signifies—all goodness, kindness, divinity or angelic power and nature, clarity, truth. He is the "light" in this story, and he lights the way for many to be healed, which is the crux of the plot.

In interesting contrast, Prot finds the light of Earth's sun too bright and wears dark glasses, and wants the blinds closed in rooms. The glaring light of the "truth" of flawed humanity hurts. Often the light catches objects in fascinating ways, creating rainbow prisms or illuminating certain parts of a room or face. When you get a chance to watch this movie, note how many times and in how many ways light is used specifically in this image system. It's brilliant (pun intended).

In the movie *What Lies Beneath* (2000), which is about a woman who sees a young woman reflected in the lake beside her home, we see another image system. It's a haunting movie with water themes, and the title nicely ties in with this theme of uncovering what really lies beneath all the visions and voices this couple experiences in their home. Water is thematic in this image system, featuring scenes with the lake, a girl drowning, the rain, water in the bathroom, steam, the tub overflowing, and others.

In *The Silence of the Lambs* (1991), we see not one specific element as the focus of the image system but a genre or type embodied in many ways. A mythic/fairy tale of "good versus evil thread" weaves throughout with allusions to labyrinth and minotaur, with a monster in a cage (Hannibal Lecter is an aberration with six fingers on each hand), with the princess at risk (Clarice is the daughter of a senator: i.e., royalty), and there are lots of little fairy tale nuances like moths and mice and spiders.

Thinking in terms of creating a larger, visual symbolism through the use of repeated types of shots, angles, colors, and other *visual* elements (that can be either blatant or subtle in the shots) can supercharge an already "good" novel. Filmmakers call these specific moments in a movie "emblematic shots."

Emblematic Shots to Highlight Theme

Think about including emblematic shots that reveal theme and motif. Is there a place your character keeps coming back to? An emotion they keep struggling with that can be symbolized by a particular scene composition and camera angle? A place where they reflect and look out on the world that can subliminally indicate their mood, self-image, or view of others? An object that they study close up?

Emblematic shots are usually placed at the beginning and end of meaningful scenes, to emphasize them, make them stand out.

Here's something you can try. Imagine taking one (only one) snapshot of your novel (not the actual physical book). This picture needs to "tell" what the core idea or theme of your story is about. Think movie poster. A movie poster has to somehow convey the feel and premise of the entire movie. Imagine showing this picture you took of your novel to a stranger and asking him what he thinks the theme or core idea is behind the photo. Ask him what symbolism comes through. Did you include symbolic elements? What colors did you choose?

Even without knowing the emotional power of each color, we all resonate similarly when it comes to colors. Can you come up with one image that can be the core of your image system? We all know a picture is worth a thousand words. If your picture can just speak a dozen key words to you, you can build an image system around it.

Positioning the Angle for Subconscious Effect

I mentioned earlier a scene in which the camera was positioned from a high angle and how it created the sense of vulnerability for the character. A high-angle shot is commonly used when trying to convey that a character feels defeated, lacking confidence, or is weak or small.

In contrast, when the camera tilts up from below to look at a character, it subconsciously implies importance and strength, with the character in a dominant position, one above others.

Just as a small child would have to look up to a tall adult, emphasizing the dominant/subordinate relationship in power and authority, so too a camera shot tilting up showing a character implies this character may be confident, assertive, powerful, domineering. This can tie in with your emblematic shots in your image system for your story.

Tilt Your Camera

Do you have a scene in which your character feels defeated or oppressed by another character? Picture that scene in your mind. Now shift the camera so that your POV character is in a lower location than your antagonist (or whatever "antagonizing" element is bearing down on her—it could even be the burning sun above her).

Instead of having both characters on equal playing ground, such as sitting at a table drinking coffee, what about having your "oppressed" character beneath a balcony or at the bottom of a set of stairs on which the antagonist is placed? What if she has to look up, strain her neck, to see him or speak to him?

Think about this character's arc for the novel. Does she start out defeated and end up victorious in her plot goal for the book? Can you think of how your earlier scenes could be "shot" at times with the camera perspective tilted to emphasize her vulnerability, impotency, feelings of inadequacy and failure?

Then picture a scene or two in the middle, as she's overcoming obstacles and faces them "head on" rather than looking up from a low position. And in the final scene or two, she can be looking down on the fruits of her victory from an elevated place, physically and emotionally.

At the Top of the World

What if you have a character who feels victorious, on top of the world? Why not place him "on top of the world" at some high place in the setting—the roof of a building or the crest of a mountain? In a scene in my novel *Intended for Harm*, Reuben, the firstborn son who loves rock climbing, ascends a mountain peak and looks out on the world, reflecting on his life as he's graduating high school. What follows is a huge moment of revelation about his place in his family and his dreams for the future (a panoramic "big picture" spread out before him). This is where he also connects with the love of his life and future wife, that moment all wrapped up with the panoramic view of the world at his feet, all his for the taking.

I chose that locale very specifically, as well as the camera shot, to get this deeper symbolism and effect. It is not only Reuben's "high moment" (pun intended) for the scene; it is also the high moment in his character arc.

Use a Final Angle to Make a Statement

Earlier we took a look at the ending moment in the classic *The Planet of the Apes* when discussing the Pull Back shot. In the shot we see Taylor on the sand, staring up at something in horror and shock. How we all gasped when the camera pulled back to reveal the Statue of Liberty.

There is one thing, though, you may not have noticed when reading the screenplay excerpt and that was the *angle* of the camera. The script reads: "He falls to his knees, buries his head in his hands. CAMERA SLOWLY DRAWS BACK AND UP to a HIGH ANGLE SHOT disclosing what Taylor has found. Half-buried in the sand and washed by the waves is the Statue of Liberty."

Why the high angle shot looking down? Wouldn't it have been much more imposing to use Taylor's prostrate POV and look *up* to this massive statue with its heavy import? I'm thinking the writer considered that. But a couple of useful things are accomplished by this angle.

First, it puts Taylor in the appropriate defeatist, vulnerable position. With this bit of knowledge, Taylor has lost all hope and has been defeated. As we've seen, this is what's implied when the camera angle looks *down* on a character. From this angle we can see both enough of the statue to recognize it and Taylor, now small. A POV shot would not have captured both. And second, w artistic angle of the statue rising up in defiance and endurance, w sand and water enwrapping it, almost giving the sense of it emer from burial. In effect, it is saying this is a truth that may not forgotten or ignored. Powerfully done, and no doubt deliberate.

So think about not just the camera shot you need to use for each segment but also keep in mind your core idea and themes for your book—your image system—and find ways to use repeated, specific angles to supercharge your story.

Chapter 14

Color and Shapes to Shape Your Novel

We all know the power of color, and books have been written in detail on the effect each color has on a person. One book that is particularly fascinating on the topic, should you be interested in going deep into color symbolism and subtext in your novel, is *If It's Purple, Someone's Gonna Die*, by Patti Bellantoni. This book helps filmmakers choose the right colors for their stories and showcases more than sixty films discussing the deliberate use of color for impact. Filmmakers have to be particular keyed in to color, since their work is so acutely visual.

Color is powerful and often completely ignored by novelists—or used randomly without purpose or just to make a fashion statement—whereas filmmakers have to be keenly aware of the subtle and often subliminal effects of different colors. Listen to what Bellantoni says:

> Films as varied as *Cabaret, Dick Tracy*, and *The Sixth Sense* all use purple to foreshadow death ... Both Gwyneth Paltrow's bedspread in *Shakespeare in Love* and Nick Cage's bedspread in *Moonstruck* are a hot orange-red, and they certainly accompanied lusty activity in those films ... A strong color elicits a strong visceral response. This, in turn, can set up an audience to anticipate a particular action.
>
> Colors indeed have their own language, which can visually help define a character arc or layer a story. In *Malcolm X*, for example, bright "look at me" red is the color that defines Malcolm's cocky small-time hoodlum years; blue, the

contemplative years in prison; and gold, his enlightened time in Mecca. Each of those colors layers the journey of this man and has a different (and cumulative) effect on the audience. Red is energizing, blue affects introspection, and golden light inspires the spiritual or enlightened. Wynn Thomas, production designer for *Malcolm X*, describes how he envisioned the film in three acts, each defined by a particular color . . .

My research suggests it is not we who decide what color can be . . . [but] I am convinced, whether we want it to or not, that it is *color* that can determine how we think and what we feel.

This can open up a whole new way of scene designing for novelists (and requires wearing yet another new hat—the production designer's). Novelists can infuse their scenes with color, whether vibrant and obvious or drab and washed out. When you have a character, in her POV, who sees the world around her as drained of color, in sepia tone, or in shades of gray, you indicate how she *feels* about her setting in that moment. Washed-out color could imply memory loss or fading emotions. They can imply a disconnect to place or people.

Filmmakers sometimes tone everything down except for one or two objects in the frame to make them stand out. A POV character can also perceive something similarly when one object appears to be brighter than anything else around it, or a glare of light shines on it, highlighting it in a symbolic way.

If you, the novelist, have an understanding of the subtle effect of color, you can purposely put these colors in your scenes—either blatantly or subtly—to help enhance the mood of the reader. Many great novelists use color in a powerful way, such as found in Toni Morrison's novel *The Bluest Eye*. In her novel the color blue is forefront in symbolism and theme.

You may not want to put that much emphasis on color, but a deliberate choice of color or tint in your scenes can be like a brush stroke of paint on a canvas used to good effect. Image systems work best when they "support and add meaning to, and not become, the point of a film" (Mercado), and so a touch of color can go far.

So take some time and research the effects of various colors on the human psyche, and play around with ideas on how you can integrate specific colors symbolically into your image systems for your novels.

Seeing your scenes with a cinematic lens involves so much more than choosing the right camera shot, as you are now beginning to see. Every segment of your scenes, if planned with deliberation and by using a filmmaker's eye, will come to life and be supercharged in ways you never imagined. Readers will be moved more powerfully by your story, and may not even know why. But you will know.

Shapes to Shape Reaction

Shapes are probably the last thing on a novelist's mind when constructing a scene or an image system for a novel. Most of us probably pay little attention to shapes. Shapes of what? Well, everything has a shape, and even if you don't think about shapes consciously, there are universal feelings that tend to go along with certain shapes, and throughout time and across cultures, shapes convey specific meaning and often symbolism.

The cross, for example, has a lot of religious symbolism connected to it. Using a cross in some fashion in a scene might imply many things, like religiousness, sacrifice, torture, or suffering. Bruce Block in his book *The Visual Story* says round shapes are "indirect, passive, romantic, organic, safe, and childlike," whereas square shapes are "direct, industrial, unnatural, adult, rigid." Triangles are "aggressive and dynamic."

Think about a character who feels stuck in a rut, her life like a treadmill. She feels as if she is going in circles, getting nowhere. Her life is a merry-go-round of colorful painted horses that are not real.

Without stating anything specifically, circles can be used in an image system throughout the novel. She could live at the end of a cul-de-sac with a circular driveway in front of her house. Her daughter could even have a pet hamster that runs in a hamster wheel, something she looks at every day and relates to. Her job could entail her doing some kind of repetitive motion that is circular (stirs sauces as a sous chef in a kitchen). With her character arc, you could have her break out of that circular rut and make a beeline toward success (whatever that means for her). By the end of the novel she might move out of that house with its circular driveway, exchange the hamster for a horse or something thing yells power and control, maybe even get a new job that feels "sharper," more "in line" with her goal for the novel.

You don't have to explain any of this to the reader, but the subconscious effect and subtle symbolism will infuse more meaning into your story.

What if your character has to make a decisive choice in the novel—something that the story builds heavily toward? He might see things not just in black and white around him but in sharp, angular shapes. Harsh light shining at the end of a dark alley where a door is illuminated can be symbolic, just as long corridors with numerous closed doors in even spacing can imply order and rigidity. Perhaps everything around him is rigid and sharp, and he is feeling forced into making a rigid decision that is either/or, and whatever decision he makes, someone will get hurt. There are no gray areas, soft places to retreat to. The world is cold and it cuts.

You can play with these types of ideas for your image systems by freewriting words: list emotions with objects, and see what shapes emerge. Filmmakers play with these concepts, so why not you?

Wrapping Up Image Systems

We've spent quite a few pages taking a look at how filmmakers create image systems. Hopefully you are starting to see how there is so much more to shooting your novel than just picking appropriate camera shots to fashion each scene. As you write or rewrite your novel, run through these exercises:

- Consider the core idea of your book. See if you can encapsulate it in a phrase or sentence. Write down words that reflect your image system. Think of how those words or ideas could be visually and symbolically portrayed throughout your novel.

- Consider how each shot in each scene will help support and convey your image system.

- Ask what the main element of each shot is, what should or should not be included in the shot, and what meaning you want conveyed.

- Think of a few emblematic shots you might use from time to time to tie in with your theme and put them in your novel.

- Rework or add a few scenes using a specific tilt of the camera for subconscious effect. Change the angle as the character changes.

- Choose one of two colors that have specific subliminal meanings and use them appropriately in your novel.

- Think where you might alter the quality of a color--either make it more vibrant or wash it out—from your POV character's perspective to reflect his mood, self-image, or life situation.

- Think of some scenes that could benefit by bringing in specific shapes to act as symbols or motifs.

Are you starting to see your novel the way a filmmaker looks at a film? I hope so. And with all these new tools in your writer's toolbox, you are well on your way to making your story visually profound and powerful.

Chapter 15

Altering Time and Perception

Films have so many fascinating ways to alter time and perception. They can use techniques to make action slow way down or even freeze (or even have only part of the frame frozen in time while other elements are still moving). They can make time appear to be moving at wild speeds. We've all seen time-lapse images of flowers opening or the sun arcing across the sky. Such is the milieu of filmmaking.

With different lenses a filmmaker can distort the image. There are fish-eye lenses that make everything round like a ball, and there are lenses that have color tints or waver like a fun-house mirror (I never thought those were fun though). In movies a singular sound can be isolated, like the ticking of a clock, or footsteps coming down the outside hallway. How many times have you heard someone's heart beating louder than a drum, accelerating as danger nears? Novelists can do all these things just as effectively in their scenes, for it's all a matter of perception.

Perception Is Always Subjective

When we keep in mind that each scene in a novel is being experienced by a POV character from her perspective, the question to ask is, just what is her state of mind? In true Roshamon style, we all witness the world around us differently. We could be on a street corner observing an accident alongside ten others, but we all might notice different things. It reminds me of the joke about a group of people asked to look through various holes in a fence and describe what they see on the other side. Up against the fence is an elephant, but because each only sees a small portion of the elephant, the descriptions are completely different. One sees something long and wiggly like a hose and another sees a massive haunch the size of a door, and so on. What we see is determined by *how* we see.

And beyond that, when asked to interpret the intentions or meanings of things we see, we all color our interpretations of events through our personal experience and knowledge. A child seeing a man talking to another man on a street might think it a friendly conversation, whereas a woman from a dangerous neighborhood might immediately recognize a shakedown, and bristle. We bring with us our past and our baggage to every situation in life. A man who feels as if he's been a victim his entire life is going to see everything with a victim mentality. His interpretation of a genuine kindness might be pity.

Earlier we looked at colors, symbols, and shapes and saw how these can be worked into an image system determined by the novel's themes and motifs. Time, light, and sound can also be deliberately manipulated to bring out the perspective of the POV character and enhance the type of mood the writer wants to achieve.

Altering Time

Earlier when discussing stationary shots I shared a passage from the novel *When Sparrows Fall*, showing how the author Meg Moseley used a Montage Shot to create a sense of skewed time for her character recovering in a hospital after an accident. Few novelists consider the quality of time and how the *perception of it* changes due to a character's circumstance. But it is a real component of our lives, and so it might just be something you will want to explore with your characters.

We all know how time almost comes to a screeching halt when waiting in an exam room for the doctor to come back with test results. And many of us women know how wacky time gets when in labor to have a baby. I remember asking my husband after the birth of our younger daughter, "Did I really only have three contractions before I pushed her out?" It sure felt like hours, and in some ways I felt like chunks of time were missing. And almost everyone wonders why time seems to ramp up speed with every passing year we grow older. Time is all subject to perception and circumstances.

A brilliant novel that explores and plays with the ebb and flow of time passing is Ian McEwan's *The Child in Time*. The book is about a man whose young daughter had been kidnapped from a market, and ever since, time seems to have stalled for him. Throughout the book McEwan plays with time—stopping it, slowing it, speeding it up, and going back in time, with present time overlapping the past. It's a fascinating book that won him the Whitbread Prize in 1987.

Show, Don't Tell, How Time Is Passing

An unimaginative novelist may say something like "for Jane, time slowed to a stop as she waited hour after hour to hear news of her son" or "Time seemed to speed up as Ralph kept glancing at the clock worried he'd never finish that report on time." Telling a reader what time feels like to a character is ineffective and lacks power. It also doesn't *show* what it looks like. How would you show time slowing down? Well, think about what it feels like to you when you are waiting anxiously for something.

We all know the expression "a watched pot never boils." It actually does, but if we stare at it for a few minutes, we start noticing lots of little things, like the way the bubbles form at first slowly on the bottom of the pot, then grow bigger and start rising faster to the surface. We might notice when the steam starts forming like wisps of ghosts and hovering over the surface of the water. We might hear the clock ticking in the background, the neighbor's dog howling. The golfers across the street laughing and whacking at golf balls (well, I lived on a golf course, so this is what I used to hear from my kitchen).

What I'm trying to show here is that our attention shifts when time seems to slow down. We start to notice things we would never notice—things we don't have the time to notice in our busy lives. But when forced to wait, we have nothing else to do but notice. We may even count the linoleum tiles over and over in a waiting room, or stare at dust motes dancing on a sunbeam.

You can convey the sense of time rolling in slow motion by altering your character's perception of time.

The same basic idea applies to speeding time up. We looked at how Montage Shots and Series of Shots can speed time up. Using clipped sentences and short words, and having a character's attention zipping from one thing to another, never able to focus long on anything, is one way to speed up time. To *him*, everything seems to be zooming around him. People are talking too fast for him to understand; chaos is reigning around him. News hits him without giving him a chance to breathe. We know what an adrenaline rush feels like in an emergency or danger situation—how the heart pounds and blood races in our ears. Writers can use the character's internal and external impressions to create a sense of quickened time.

Skewed Time

If you haven't watched the movie *Memento* (2000), I highly recommend it. I've concluded after watching this film numerous times that the screenwriter-director Christopher Nolan must have first written the scenes in chronological order, then printed the script, took a pair of scissors, and cut it all apart and put it all in backward order. Or something like that. The black-and-white scenes are shown in chronological order, while the color scenes work backward in time, and at the end of the movie the two sets create a circular completion, meeting at the end and piecing everything, finally, together.

Why was the movie done like this? Because it's about a man who has short-term memory loss and whose sense of time is radically constricted. Since he can only recall short passages of time, aside from his long-term memories, the scenes are choppy and short, and cut off in the middle of what is happening. His character, Leonard Shelby, has to tattoo hints on his body, and leave himself notes and Polaroid snapshots in order to help him solve this murder mystery that he seems to be involved in but can't remember.

Creating the Same Effects in Your Novel

So think about your characters. Are there moments in your novel when someone is waiting expectantly for something important to arrive or happen? Are there situations in which your character is slammed by an event that leaves him reeling, unable to process what is going on around him?

Look for those moments in your scenes and play with the character's perception of time. Slowing down time for a character does not equate to slowing down the novel's pacing. In fact, slowed time, when done well, adds tremendous tension, which keeps readers turning pages as fast as they can to find out how this tense situation will resolve.

Bringing Time into Your Image System

In the movie *Unbreakable* (2000), written by M. Night Shyamalan, near the end when Elijah Price, the antagonist, reveals to the hero David Dunn through a touch of their hands that he had set up and caused the numerous catastrophic disasters around the city (planting bombs for example) that caused hundreds of deaths, images of each disaster are shown in a creative jagged sequence of time. The film sequence only took less than a minute, but it stuck with me for years.

The shots are void of color except for bits of blue on Elijah, and Shyamalan uses an interesting effect by having portions of each clip speed up and move on to the next shot. It's one of the most important moments in the whole movie, and so what is revealed in a scant few seconds needs to have impact.

And Shyamalan does this by altering time in a subtle way, as well as bringing in color splashes to make these emblematic shots. They are also, interestingly, shot from a high angle looking down, and tilted so they are skewed, reflecting his character's warped egocentric sense of superiority and entitlement—it's his calling to do these evil things, but he is whacked, and so the camera angle enhances this.

Great elements of an image system and all in just a few seconds of film.

Here's how the scene reads in the script I was able to access online, although in the movie, Elijah says, "I think this is where we shake hands" and he extends his hand for Dunn to take, knowing he will then "see" the truth, finally.

```
Elijah has a newspaper on his lap. He holds it
up.

There's a drawing on the front page. It's a
hooded figure shielding two huddled children
behind him.

                 ELIJAH
                 (soft)
            It has begun.
```

David stares quietly at the sketch of himself.

> ELIJAH
> When I saw it this morning,
> I felt a part of the world
> again.

Elijah looks down at the newspaper.

David hesitates and then reaches forward.

He reaches past the paper... And TOUCHES ELIJAH'S ARM.

FLASHCUT: AN AIRPORT GATE. ELIJAH IS STANDING AT THE WINDOW LOOKING OUT ONTO THE AIRFIELD. HE'S CRYING.

SIRENS START SOUNDING THROUGHOUT THE AIRPORT.

WAITING PASSENGERS START GETTING UP AND MOVING TO THE WINDOWS.

> MAN
> What's going on?

Elijah speaks to no one in particular as he stares out the window with tortured eyes.

> ELIJAH
> A plane just crashed.

> CUT TO:

FLASH CUT: ELIJAH AND AN ELDERLY MAN IN A UNIFORM ARE SEATED IN A HOTEL BAR.

> ELDERLY MAN
> I've worked here twenty-five
> years. I know all its secrets.

> ELIJAH
> Secrets?

> ELDERLY MAN
> (whispers)
> Like if there was ever a
> fire on floors one, two, or
> three... Everyone in this
> hotel would be burned alive.

ELIJAH LOOKS UP FROM HIS DRINK.

CUT TO:

FLASHCUT: ELIJAH LEAVES THE ENGINEERING ROOM
OF AN AMTRAK TRAIN. HE PASSES THE ENGINEER WHO
HAS JUST ARRIVED WITH COFFEE.

> ENGINEER
> Passengers aren't allowed in
> there.

Elijah doesn't answer and doesn't turn around
as he exits train 177.

SLAM CUT BACK TO PRESENT:

David takes two unsteady steps back. Elijah
has tears in his eyes as he gazes down at the
newspaper. He looks up to David.

By paying attention to how time flows for you, at different moments of your life, you can pick up ideas you can use in your novels. But don't leave time out of the equation. Great moments in film are often the ones in which time slows down or has a jagged cut to it.

Chapter 16

The Sound of . . . Sound

In the book *Cinematic Storytelling* by Jennifer Van Sijll, we read this about sound: "Sound effects are as much the purview of the writer as are visual symbols. . . . Sound effects can also suggest an extended aural metaphor. They can add layers to a film that are hard to achieve in other ways. Sound effects can be obvious or quite subtle. They can intentionally draw attention to themselves or manipulate with stealth. They can expose, disguise, suggest, establish, or reveal."

Exploring the Perception of Sound

Writers are encouraged to infuse their novels with sensory details to better immerse the reader in time and place, and sound is a powerful sense. I've often envisioned the day when readers will be able to read my novels with my original soundtrack playing as they "turn pages" on their iPad, the music adjusting in speed to the speed of the reader so that the climactic symphonic rise pairs with the high moments of my scenes. I've often thought of talking to some of my Silicon Valley neighbors who design apps to work with me to create a prototype, but I imagine someone is already working on this.

Movie scores affect viewers powerfully, eliciting strong emotions that can make moviegoers cry and despair or feel their hearts soaring with joy. There are movies I watch in which, when a certain piece of music or song begins to play, I start blubbering—like at the ending of *Fly Away Home* when Mary Chapin Carpenter starts singing "Ten Thousand Miles." I get choked up just writing this, and that song is on my iPhone and has been played at least a thousand times over a thousand miles. I probably would have loved this song regardless of its place in the movie, but when pairing a tremendously emotional movie with a gorgeous, meaningful song, an exponential emotional explosion occurs. But until the day novels are paired with their own music scores that play while being read, writers will have to make do with other ways to portray music and sounds in their novels.

Many novelists mention various sounds occurring around their characters in scenes, and often to great effect. Good writers will evoke that unique sense of place by the clink of glasses, the tinkle of happy banter, the drip of a faucet in an abandoned building, the screech of tires from a car racing away from the scene of a crime. If you haven't spent much time thinking about sounds and their potential effect on a scene, I would recommend you do so.

Filmmakers classify sounds into three categories.

- First are natural sounds, ones that would normally be found in a particular environment, and those are the ones most novelists include in their scenes.

- Second are "expressive" sounds, and those are normal sounds altered by the perception of the character. For example, a phone could begin ringing louder and louder until the character either notices it or starts to scream in anger. Again, it's a matter of perception. In a novel, a harried new mother could be trying to soothe her crying baby, whose cries seem to grow louder and louder, along with the TV blaring and someone banging on the door, and even the tea kettle screaming. All this can be amplified into "expressive" sounds to portray her tension, exasperation, and growing panic.

- Third are classified as "surreal" sounds. These externalize a character's inner thoughts, nightmares, wishes, or dreams. They are not real sounds; they are imagined. Think of a man who does something stupid and hears everyone laughing at him although their faces are emotionless. Novelists can show their characters perceiving these surreal sounds, for *their characters* hear them, whether they are real or not.

Emblematic Sounds

Sounds can be emblematic. The hum of a mosquito can be deafening and a recurring motif in an image system. Even the jangle of keys can be terrifying, as seen in the opening scene of the movie *E. T.* as the terrified little extraterrestrial runs from the men chasing him. You've probably watched movies in which all the sound is muted except for one isolated sound.

I took particular note of sound the first time I saw *The Fellowship of the Ring* (2001) at the moment right after Gandalf falls with the Balrog into the depths of Moria. Peter Jackson, director, not only slowed the film action way down as Strider grabbed Frodo and forced him out of the mines into bright sunlight but also muted every sound—even Frodo's loud cries, which are evident by the Close-Up on his face and all the loud noise of a gazillion orcs coming at them—except for the *swoosh* of the arrows flying past them all.

The sound engineer did a brilliant job with this effect. There is a softness to the sound, as one arrow then another flies past their heads, which helps to skew time and also show Frodo's numbness to what has just happened. He can barely hear anything around him as his grief and horror strike hard. A beautiful cinematic use of sound.

Novelists Can Do It Too

This isn't all that hard for novelists to emulate. By describing just how a character is perceiving the sounds around her, writers can essentially do the same. One sound out of many can be singled out, and that sound can even be symbolic or work as a metaphor as part of the image system. A loud heartbeat can override all other noises.

You may have seen this done in movies. A spaceman in a spacesuit is trying to fix something outside a station orbiting a planet hearing his heart beating hard. As danger approaches, the heart rate speeds up, gets louder. It's all he can hear. Sounds underwater are distorted and muted, and a drunk or drugged character may hear sounds that aren't really there.

Think of ways sounds can be used as symbols or motifs in your novel. A ringing bell can be part of a pastoral landscape coming from a church nearby, but it can also mark time, and symbolize time running out.

Foley artists are the ones responsible for sound effects in a film. They usually begin their work by watching the film to determine which sounds need to be replaced or added. Novelists can do similarly as they work on revisions. I laugh sometimes at TV shows that use repeated trademark sounds perfunctorily, such as when a medieval village scene begins and the expected chicken crowing occurs. Or when horses are shown, one always knickers or whinnies. Foley artists try to add in those natural sounds to bring more realism to the scene. There might be added crowd noises, the sound of glasses clinking, the tick of an old grandfather clock, footsteps that need to go along with the movement of characters.

Which might make a novelist think:

- How much attention should be paid to sound in my novel?

- How can I think like a Foley artist and go through to add sounds the characters would notice and that would enhance each scene?

- Are there places where it would be appropriate for me to use enhanced, expressive, distorted, and/or surreal sounds to add tension?

Randy Thom, a Foley artist who has received numerous Academy Award nominations for sound in feature films, says, "Amplified reality is the basic goal in action-adventure and sci-fi sequences. Forget what real sounds are like and start thinking about what it would feel like in a nightmare. . . . like an engine sounding like a growling beast. The essential emotional quality of the sound is virtually all that matters."

He makes this succinct point: "Storytelling is about making connections between characters, places, ideas, and experiences. It isn't enough for a sound to be merely loud or high fidelity, or digital. It needs to remind you of, resonate with, other sounds, places, feelings, in other times."

This is good advice for novelists seeking to add touches of sound with a Foley artist's flair. So as you create and revise the scenes in your novel, try to wear this hat for a while and infuse your story with sounds in cinematic fashion. Just one more cinematic secret that will help supercharge your novel.

Chapter 17

Movies in Our Characters' Heads

In novels, we are almost always in our characters' heads. An entire story is told from the viewpoints of the various characters, colored by how they perceive and experience their world and the story that unfolds in the plot. In real life, we spend a lot of time thinking. Often—sometimes more than often—we spend immersed in imagining. We imagine our futures: what our future spouse might be like, what our dream job might entail, what the future might hold in every which way. Every great achievement and invention in history began as an idea or dream in someone's head. "Dreaming" like this is common to everyone and a large part of life and who we are.

Novelists can show their characters thinking about something, and they do this a lot. And that is often a great way to reveal character and fill in bits of backstory. But thinking about something isn't quite the same as "dreaming" about it. I am not talking about the kind of dreaming we do when we're asleep, and a whole lot of interesting camera shots and cinematic technique can be used to portray the actual dream state. I'm talking about those moments when we get lost in our imaginings. It might be simply summed up as daydreaming. And when we daydream, it's as if we are playing out a live-action scene from a movie in our heads, with ourselves as the star of the show.

So how might a novelist play out a scene in a character's head—whether it be a memory or something he's imagining, perhaps a dream for the future?

We're going to take a look at *Marathon Man*, a conspiracy thriller written by William Goldman (*The Princess Bride* author) in 1974, which shows beautifully how a novelist can use this cinematic technique. Goldman began as a novelist, and wrote five novels and had three plays on Broadway before he turned his attention to screenwriting. Novelists who are also screenwriters understand and utilize cinematic secrets to best effect in their storytelling, for they understand both how a scene needs to visually unfold on the big screen as well as how to translate the desired effect into prose in their novels.

Take a Look at Novelists Who Are Also Screenwriters

Looking at and comparing a novel and screenplay written by the same author gives some great insights into cinematic technique and how to "adapt" camera shots to supercharge your novel. We took a look at Michael Crichton's *Jurassic Park* earlier to see how one of his Establishing Shots portrayed in the film was conveyed in a scene in his novel. There are numerous writers who are successful at both film and novel writing, and if you want to learn best how to infuse cinematic technique into your fiction, you may want to take some time to look at both their novels and the corresponding screenplays.

Of course, screenplays rarely reflect a novel precisely. Often scenes and plot elements that work in a novel don't work well in a ninety-minute encapsulation of a story. Adapting a novel and turning it into a screenplay is a challenging endeavor, and not many novels are suitable for such transformation. But screenwriters who write their novels cinematically make it easy for adaptation, as they have already constructed the scenes in their novel to play out and feel like movie scenes.

The Movies That Play in Our Heads

The movie *Marathon Man* (1976) opens with archival footage of marathon champion Abebe Bikila from the 1964 Olympics. Tension builds with pitch-bending strings as the older black-and-white footage fades into graduate student Thomas Babington "Babe" Levy (Dustin Hoffman) jogging around the Central Park Reservoir in New York. While he runs, we get intercuts of Nazi war criminal Dr. Szell getting diamonds out of a safe deposit box.

However, In Goldman's novel, we get to go deep in Levy's head— something that makes novels so different and often more powerful than movies—to understand right away just who Levy is and what his hopes and dreams are. Instead of Goldman "telling" all this with narrative in the opening of the book, he shows it in a creative cinematic way—the way we often do in our heads: through imagining. Look how much we learn about Levy by watching the scene playing out inside his head.

So at half-past five Levy ran. Clearly he was faster than anyone around, so if you were a casual observer it would have been logical to assume that this rather tallish, sort of slender fellow with the running style not unreminiscent of a goose covered ground really quite well.

But you had to consider his daydreams.

He was going to run the marathon. Like Nurmi. Like the already mythical Nurmi. Years from now, all across the world, track bugs would agonize over who was the greatest . . . some of them would argue, "No one would ever run the final five miles the way Levy ran them," and others would counter that by the time the last five miles came, Nurmi would be so far ahead, it wouldn't matter how fast Levy ran them, and so the debate would rage, expert against expert, down the decades.

For Levy was not going to be a marathon man; anyone could be that if you just devoted your life to it. No, he was going to be *the* marathon man. . . .

Right now he only had the B.Litt. he'd won at Oxford, and could race but fifteen miles without fatigue. But give him a few more years and he would be both PhD and Champion. And the crowds would sing out "*Lee*-vee, *Lee*-vee," sending him on to undreamed-of triumphs as now sports fans shouted, "*Dee*-fense" as they urged on their heroes.

"*Lee*-vee, *Lee*-vee—"

And they wouldn't care about how awkwardly he might run. It wouldn't matter to them that he was over six feet tall and under a hundred and fifty pounds, no matter how many milkshakes he downed per day in an effort to move up from skinny to slender.

"*Lee*-vee! *Lee*-vee!—"

It wouldn't bother them that he had a stupid cowlick and the face of an Indiana farmer, that even after spending three years in England he still had the expression of someone you just knew would buy the Brooklyn Bridge if you offered him the chance. He was beloved by few, known by none save, thank God for Doc,

Doc. But that would change. Oh yes, oh yes.

"*LEE-VEE . . . LEEEEEEE-VEE.*"

There he was now, up ahead and running with the firm knowledge that no one could ever conquer him, except possibly Mercury. Tireless, fabled, arrogant, unbeatable, the Flying Finn himself, Nurmi.

Levy picked up his pace.

The end of the race was still miles off, but now was the greatest test, the test of the heart.

Levy picked up his pace again.

Levy was gaining.

The half-million people lining the course could not believe it. They screamed, they surged almost out of control. It could not be happening but there it was—*Levy was gaining on Nurmi.*

And the race inside Levy's head continues until he's mentally interrupted by his chronic toothache, followed by thoughts of needing to see a dentist, which then goes into other thoughts about his job, segueing into other details important to setting up the premise and overarching plot.

Daydreaming Is a Part of Life

I imagine if we really paid attention, we'd see how we spend numerous hours of each day imagining ourselves in scenes—whether events that have happened to us or imaginary ones, like the one Goldman created for his character Levy.

Novelists often go deep into POV, showing their character thinking about things and reacting to what is happening in the present scene. Using deep POV is not only common but considered the way great novels are now mostly written. However, often these internalized thoughts and responses, although frequently effective, are not cinematic. And there's nothing wrong with that.

But what if you chose two or three scenes in which your character is thinking about something and instead played out her thoughts cinematically, the way Goldman did, and the way we often do in real life?

Have your character envision a "what if" and play out her dream in her head with her in the starring role. Or if it's crucial she reflect on a past hurt or a key moment in her childhood that gives an important clue in the novel, replay it in her head, even have her watch herself and notice things she may have missed before. But make it cinematic, visual. Let the reader "watch" her in that scene.

Watch That Backstory

You could consider this backstory or a flashback, and so you want to be careful you don't spend so much time in the "past recollection" that you are neglecting the present scene action. You don't want to start your novel in one place and time, only to jerk the reader to some other past situation. You want to ground your reader right away in the "now" moment the novel opens with. That's why so many instructors say "no backstory in the first thirty pages" of a novel. Notice Goldman doesn't go into backstory. He has a short mention of a degree Levy got at Oxford. And he creatively describes his character while staying in Levy's POV (which is cleverly done). But the rest is Levy dreaming while he's running through Central Park.

The movie, in my opinion, could have shown this better. Rather that start with the film clip of Bikila winning the marathon, then just showing Levy running, there could have been clips in a montage of Levy's dream win interspersed with his pounding the pavement. But I didn't get to write the screenplay . . .

Play Out the Dreams

Since it's so important to make clear your characters' core needs and dreams in a novel, think about using this cinematic technique of "playing out" that dream or need in their heads in cinematic fashion. With a mystery/suspense novel, writers have plenty of opportunities for their detectives or others investigating and searching for clues to picture what may have happened at a crime scene or in an attempt to outthink a killer or kidnapper.

Instead of just having your character think about all the clues, why not try shooting the "what if" in your character's head? It will help not just him but your reader to visualize it so much better. And it will give a lasting cinematic quality to your scene that will not be so easily forgotten.

Chapter 18

Conclusion

"Lights, camera . . . action!"

Hopefully those three little words have much more meaning for you now. While looking through the camera lens, you've put on a lot of hats—those of the screenwriter, director, film editor, filmmaker, and more, and perhaps you've gotten a better picture of what goes into the making of a film.

You've seen how all the primary camera shots are used in movies and how they might transfer over into a novel's scenes. And you've learned a little about the filmmaker's eye—how to see beyond the shot to theme, meaning, and symbolism to enhance the overarching story. Hopefully you now have a new "lens" to look through as you consider your novel, and you are eager to start using those great tools now overflowing from your writer's toolbox. You now have a greater sense of what it means to "show, don't tell." Yes, you are really ready to "shoot your novel."

New Concepts, New Ways of Seeing Your Story

Understanding how scenes in films are made of segments strung together can help novelists in constructing their scenes. Thinking of where a POV character's "camera" is and what it is doing may be a new concept to many but opens vast possibilities perhaps never before imagined. Purposefully "setting up" scenes from specific angles and using emblematic shots that consider color, sound, and lighting can aid writers in driving home their themes and evoking powerful emotional reactions. In this age in which we are inundated with visual stories, novelists do well to infuse their novels with cinematic technique.

That's not to say that every scene in a novel should play out like a movie. But writers looking to supercharge their stories and take them from flat to dynamic, from good to unforgettable, can borrow and adapt these powerful cinematic secrets. There is no better way to supercharge your writing than by "shooting" your novel.

About the Author

C. S. Lakin is passionate about writing and helping writers see success in their writing journey. She's the author of twenty novels in various genres, which includes her seven-book fantasy series The Gates of Heaven and numerous novels in her historical Western romance Front Range series (under pen name Charlene Whitman). She works full-time as a copyeditor and writing coach.

Her award-winning blog for writers, Live Write Thrive, is an excellent resource for both fiction and nonfiction writers, with hundreds of posts on craft, marketing, and writing for life. She also puts out a newsletter to her readers with tips and insights on how to be productive and find success as a writer.

In addition to editing and proofreading, Lakin critiques more than two hundred manuscripts a year. If you've never had your work critiqued, you may be unaware of many weaknesses in your writing and story structure. Consider getting your scene outline or first chapters critiqued to help you see what needs work. You can learn more about her critique services and pricing at her website Critique My Manuscript.

Did you find this writing craft book helpful? The best way to thank a writer is to leave a positive, honest review. Please take the time to leave a review on Amazon.com for this book that will help other writers discover the secret to writing an unforgettable novel!

Novels Excerpted

Alone, by Lisa Gardner, copyright © 2005 by Lisa Gardner, published by Bantam Books, a division of Random House, Inc.

Falling Man, by Don DeLillo, copyright © 2007 by Don DeLillo, published by Scribner, a division of Simon & Schuster

Jurassic Park, by Michael Crichton, paperback version copyright © 1993 by Michael Crichton, published by Ballantine Books, an imprint of Random House Publishing Group

Kill Me If You Can, by James Patterson and Marshall Karp, copyright © 2011 by James Patterson, published by Little, Brown and Company, a division of Hachette Book Group

Let the Great World Spin, by Colum McCann, copyright © 2009 by Colum McCann, published by Random House Publishing Group

Marathon Man, by William Goldman, copyright © 1994 by William Goldman, published by Dell Books

Nineteen Minutes, by Jodi Picoult, copyright © 2007 by Jodi Picoult, published by Atria Books, a division of Simon & Schuster

Peace Like a River, by Leif Enger, copyright © 2001 by Leif Enger, published by Grove Press, an imprint of Grove/Atlantic, Inc.

Predator, by Terri Blackstock, copyright © 2010 by Terri Blackstock, published by Zondervan, an imprint of HarperCollins Publishers

Shibumi, by Trevanian, copyright © 1983 by Trevanian, published by Ballantine Books, an imprint of Random House Publishing Group

Sixth Man, by David Baldacci, copyright © 2011 by Columbus Rose, Ltd., published by Grand Central Publishing, a division of Hachette Book Group

The Constant Gardener, by John Le Carré, copyright © 2005 by John Le Carré, published by Scribner, an imprint of Simon & Schuster, Inc.

Recommended Bibliography

The Filmmaker's Eye, by Gustav Mercado

Cinematic Storytelling, by Jennifer Van Sijll

If It's Purple, Someone's Gonna Die, by Patti Belantoni

The Conversations: Walter Murch and the Art of Editing Film, by Michael Ondaatje

First Cut: Conversations with Film Editors, by Gabriella Oldham

In the Blink of an Eye, by Walter Murch

The Five C's of Cinematography: Motion Picture Filming Techniques, by Joseph Mascelli

Film Directing Shot by Shot, by Steven D. Katz

Master Shots (Volumes I and II), by Christopher Kenworthy

Film Lighting, by Kris Malkiewicz

Don't miss any books in
The Writer's Toolbox series!

These books cover nearly everything you need to know to write great fiction and structure solid stories!

Writing the Heart of Your Story: The Secret to Crafting an Unforgettable Novel

Shoot Your Novel: Cinematic Techniques to Supercharge Your Writing

The 12 Key Pillars of Novel Construction: Your Blueprint for Building a Solid Story

The 12 Key Pillars Workbook

5 Editors Tackle the 12 Fatal Flaws of Fiction Writing

Say What? The Fiction Writer's Handy Guide to Grammar, Punctuation, and Word Usage

Crank It Out! The Surefire Way to Become a Super-Productive Writer

Layer Your Novel: The Innovative Method for Plotting Your Scenes

Here's a sneak peek at
The 12 Key Pillars of Novel Construction:

The 12 Key Pillars of Novel Construction

Think about Construction

Most writers—particular beginning novelists—get tripped up and struggle with pretty much the same things when attempting to construct a novel. And rightly so. Writing a novel is not easy, despite what some say (and usually it's the people who have never written one who say that).

Unfortunately, I get the feeling, when I start in on various novel critiques, that the client I am trying to help did not think it important to first take the time to learn as much about novel construction as possible. Many manuscripts I critique seem to be written off the top of the head, the scenes just thrown onto the page without forethought.

So few novels seem to be actually *constructed*. Or if they are constructed, they are done faultily, doomed to failure (and often by the end of page 1).

The concept of construction is nothing new. However, I'm a building contractor's wife, and since I've spent many long hours nailing siding according to blueprint nailing specifications and cutting two-by-fours carefully to the sixteenth of an inch in order for all the studs to fit precisely in framing up a house, the word *construction* has a rich and evocative meaning for me. As does the word *blueprint*. Any builder who attempts to construct a complex house without engineered plans would be rightly called a fool.

The Odds Are You *Won't* Accidently Write a Perfect Novel

Of course, "building" a faulty novel won't endanger anyone's life (we hope), but it can sure be a lesson in frustration and aggravation, and a very big waste of time. That's not to say practicing writing is a waste of time; it's not. But, well, it can be if there is no end to the means.

If you write randomly and learn nothing, does it really benefit you? Sure, exercises like participating in nanwrimo (National Novel Writing Month) teach you admirable things like discipline, perseverance, stick-to-itiveness (yep, that really is a word!). But those qualities alone will not improve your writing skills or turn you into a novelist.

To use a different analogy, I could spend three hours pouring random ingredients into a big bowl and stirring, stirring, stirring. That doesn't guarantee that when I pour it into a pan and bake it, a delicious and beautiful cake will emerge from my oven. In fact, it's akin to the old line about setting a million monkeys down in front of typewriters and believing that eventually, some thousands of years down the line, one monkey will accidentally and perfectly produce the Bible word for word.

Truthfully? Most novels I critique are a lot like that bowl of random elements. And it's really hard to take a finished product like that yucky baked cake and turn it into something palatable, let alone delicious. If only the writer took the time to find a solid, time-tested recipe and followed that. A recipe is like . . . a blueprint. Which brings me back around to building construction.

How Much Time Do You Want to Waste?

If you haven't figured me out yet, let me just say I am all about *not* wasting time. Life is short, too short. Some of you have read my polite rants on plotting and learning this craft well so as to *not* waste time. Time is the most precious and valuable commodity we have. It is a limited resource, and life demands we spend the increments of time on so many things. If I wrote down everything I did in a day, every tiny little thing I did requiring a measure of time, I would probably be shocked. We have to divide up our time into little bits in order to take care of the many responsibilities we handle.

That's not saying we should be neurotic and never waste a second. But why waste time if we don't need to? And when it comes to writing novels, I am astounded by how much time writers are willing to waste, basically stirring that bowl of ingredients day after day (and even year after year), without first taking the time to find the right recipe and then following the directions using the required ingredients.

I know I'm jumping back and forth here between baking a cake and building a house. But building and constructing and baking are all about the same thing. Some of you can't relate to being on a construction crew and framing up a house. But most of you can relate to following a recipe and cooking something, right? Even if it's just one of those box cakes that say all you have to add are water, an egg, and a half-cup of oil. Simple, but you still need to do what it says or your cake will come out awful.

All in all, for just about every task we do in life, we follow some sort of instructions in order to succeed. Change the oil in your car. Upload a picture to Facebook. So why is it so many writers think they don't need to follow instructions when constructing a novel?

Different Techniques but the Same Engineering Principles

Here's one reason: there are lots of different blueprints (or recipes) out there regarding novel construction. So many different techniques and styles. Some writers throw their hands up thinking that since that's the case, it really doesn't matter what method they use. Clearly anything goes. You take all those basic ingredients of plot, character, dialog, and theme and throw them into the mixer and, voila! A novel!

Well, here's the thing. If you ask great writing instructors about this, they will tell you there are time-tested rules or principles to novel-building. Just as with a house. There are myriads of houses—of different sizes, shapes, layouts—many made of very different materials. But there are basic principles that tie in with the natural laws of physics and engineering.

Materials have stress loads and limitations. Those factors have to be considered by the engineer designing the blueprints. And the building contractor has to follow those blueprints to ensure the house will be sturdy and safe.

In the same manner, novel construction requires acknowledging the scope, function, and limitations of all its elements. There are structures that have proven to be solid and others flawed. Regardless of genre, writer's voice, or premise, there are some construction basics that apply to pretty much every novel—unless you are going with something experimental and you don't really care if the whole thing collapses. But most novelists want their novels to stand the test of time and stand up to the scrutiny of their target audience. They attempt to "build a house" their fans can inhabit and enjoy, which is the dwelling place of their story.

You can already see where this is leading to, I'm sure. In *Shoot Your Novel* I had you put on your filmmaker's hat to be able to learn helpful cinematic technique. With this method, you get to wear a hard hat! Yes, bricks are going to fly! But my aim is to help you become a terrific building and engineer, and by learning what these twelve essential pillars are and how they support your story, you will become proficient in novel construction. No more throwing a bunch of materials into the mixer and hoping a great book comes out. Novel construction doesn't have to be (and shouldn't be) guesswork.

Which gets back to my earlier point about wasting time. The main point to all this is to avoid wasting time and energy stirring and stirring and producing nothing palatable. By following established blueprints for novel construction, you can use your time wisely and write a terrific novel and still have time to do all those other things you want and need to do in your life, including stopping and smelling the roses.

So get ready to load up that tool belt with construction tools as we look deeply at the twelve key pillars of novel construction.

Your Novel as a House

Take a moment to imagine your novel as a house. Or more like an ancient Greek building, like the Parthenon. Made completely of marble, heavy marble—including the massive roof. Then imagine how strong those columns have to be to support such a gargantuan weight. One replacement column recently installed on the Parthenon was weighed in at around fifty tons! Although no one has ever weighed the entire Parthenon, architects state that just the cast iron that supports the dome of the US Capitol building in Washington, DC, has been estimated at around 8.9 *million* pounds. It's hard to believe any structure made of any materials could hold up such weight.

But these buildings have remained standing through centuries, without collapsing. Which attests to the strength and reliability of the materials used in these structures—as well as the brilliance of the architects that designed them.

Novelists are architects too—architects of story. Just as a level, appropriate, and rock-solid foundation is needed as a base to any lasting building, a writer must have a similarly strong and informed foundation in order to write strong novels. Upon such a foundation a great novel can be built. But as much as the right foundation is essential, the structural integrity of the entire project must be exact or the "building" will collapse.

So if we liken the completed novel to the roof—the very heavy marble roof—then consider the pillars supporting the roof as the key to success. We want "fifty-ton" columns to support our roof so it will not only look sturdy but stand the test of time.

Not Just Pretty to Look At

Aesthetics are a main concern in construction. Architects are praised for designing a beautiful, captivating house or monument. But structural integrity cannot be sacrificed on the altar of beauty. They go hand in hand. I've always thought it a shame that those exquisitely crafted ice or sand sculptures I've seen constructed as entries in a competition were so temporal. One wave . . . or one day in a warm room . . . and those magnificent works of art disappeared. Although I understand the joy experienced in the act of creating, it seems a waste to put that much effort out to create something so beautiful and detailed, only to watch it melt before your eyes.

Some novels are like those ephemeral sculptures—adorned with lovely writing, presenting an intriguing premise, and perfectly edited to present the appearance of a great novel. But when examined under the scrutiny of a "construction engineer" (read: savvy reader), the pillars that support the story are flimsy and weak. Collapse is inevitable, and probably has already occurred—even in the first few pages. And the sad thing is the writer can't see it. Or upon learning the story has collapsed, can't understand how in the world that could have happened.

She might say, "But I had a great idea. I worked out a clever, fresh plot. I have great characters. So what went wrong?"

Take the Requisite Construction Course

I'm married to a building contractor, who is a stickler for structure. He pores endlessly over blueprints before beginning to construct a house, often finding mistakes the engineers have made. He understands structure so well that he can spot any little thing that might compromise the support of the house. It could be a prescribed nail pattern for a sheer wall, or the thickness of the rebar noted to be used in the concrete forms.

This type of knowledge and deep understanding of construction is not something that can be learned by watching a few TV shows or skimming through some do-it-yourself books found at The Home Depot. A lot of this kind of knowledge comes from on-the-job experience, which is mostly how my husband learned his skills—assisting, watching, and questioning the expert building contractors he worked with for years. Hands-on experience coupled with diligent "book" learning.

And so too, writers, to construct solid, lasting novels, need both "hands-on" experience as well as "book" learning. I use the term "book learning" as a catch-all for any type of informational instruction that is not a part of actual practice—which involves sitting down and writing. This can be knowledge gained by attending workshops (online or in person), conferences, or writing retreats, or reading blog posts and articles on writing, studying writing craft books, and working with writing groups and critique partners. And now here, with this book, you'll be given some great "book learning" you can couple with your "hands-on" experience.

An Introduction to the 12 Key Pillars

I've come up with a "construction" of my own, to make teaching these essentials easy. I mentioned earlier about the need to carefully plan a novel in advance, just as a builder would do when getting ready to build a house. In like manner, we're going to look deeply at twelve key pillars novelists need to learn to build in order to construct a solid novel.

The primary four—likened to the important corner supports of a building—provide the main framework upon which the entire story rests. The other eight secondary pillars add the additional strength needed to hold up the novel. Once a writer sets in place the four solid corner pillars, the other eight can be fashioned and positioned. But without those four major supports, the entire structure will collapse.

The Four Corner Pillars

Since these four pillars are the big supports of your story, we'll be spending the most time on them. These are what I see lacking in many of the novels I critique, and usually are the primary cause of construction failure. A novel that ignores or belittles the importance of any of these four pillars will be doomed to fail. Every time. They are as follows:

- **Concept . . . with a Kicker**
- **Conflict . . . with High Stakes**
- **Protagonist . . . with a Goal**
- **Theme . . . with a Heart**

We'll be going deep into these four pillars, and I'll explain why they are so important and how they act as supports in your story. And after that, we'll explore the other eight pillars. Here they are:

- **Plot and Subplots . . . in a String of Scenes**
- **Secondary Characters . . . with Their Own Needs**
- **Setting . . . with a Purpose**
- **Tension . . . Ramped to the Max**
- **Dialog . . . Compressed and Essential**
- **Voice . . . Unique for Each Character**
- **Writing Style . . . Concise and Specific**
- **Motifs . . . for Cohesion and Depth**

You Have to Pass Every Inspection

Builders are required to pass numerous inspections before the house they're building can ultimately get "signed off." If anywhere along the line the inspector finds something wrong—not up to code, or in conflict with the blueprints—the builder has to fix it in order to pass that inspection.

So here's the fun part! With each of the 12 pillars, you will get an inspection checklist of 12 sets of essential questions. These are questions you will ask yourself about your novel and must be answered solidly to ensure you have a strong pillar. I'll provide a checklist in this book, as well as the link to the pdfs that you can download and print out (as often as needed) to use as worksheets to help you firm up your pillars.

At the end of this course you'll have 12 checklists, with a total of 144 questions. By answering all those key questions (which are meant to ensure you've done a proper job constructing each pillar), you will know you have built well. A great tool you'll be able to use on each and every novel you construct!

The 12 Key Pillars of Novel Construction **is available in print and as a Kindle ebook.**

Printed in Great Britain
by Amazon